D1220903

To God be the glory—great things He hath done!
So loved He the world that He gave us His Son,
Who yielded His life an atonement for sin
And opened the Lifegate that all may go in.

Great things He hath taught us, great things He hath done,
And great our rejoicing thru Jesus the Son;
But purer and higher and greater will be
Our wonder, our transport, when Jesus we see.

Praise the Lord, Praise the Lord,
Let the earth hear His voice!
Praise the Lord, Praise the Lord,
Let the people rejoice!
O come to the Father thru Jesus the Son,
And give Him the glory—great things He hath done!

—Fanny J. Crosby

TRANSFORMED

BY HIS

GLORY

CHARLES C. RYRIE

VICTOR BOOKS®

A DIVISION OF SCRIPTURE PRESS PUBLICATIONS INC.
USA CANADA ENGLAND

The Scripture quotations in this book are primarily the author's para-
phrases, drawn from the *New American Standard Bible* (NASB), © The
Lockman Foundation 1960, 1962, 1963, 1968, 1971, 1972, 1973, 1975,
1977; the *Holy Bible, New International Version* (NIV), © 1973, 1978,
1984, International Bible Society, used by permission of Zondervan
Bible Publishers; and the *King James Version* (KJV).

Jacket Designer: Scott Rattray

Library of Congress Cataloging-in-Publication Data

Ryrie, Charles Caldwell, 1925–
    Transformed by His glory / Charles Ryrie.
        p.   cm.
    ISBN 0-89693-696-1
    1. Glory of God. 2. Christian life—1960-   I. Title.
BT180.G6R97   1990
231'.4–dc20   90-33533
                                                                  CIP

1 2 3 4 5 6 7 8 9 10 Printing/Year 94 93 92 91 90

Contents

A Brief Word from the Author

I thought you might be interested to know how this book came to be. I've had in the back of my mind for years that the glory of God would be an important topic to write about. And a practical one as well.

But how to do it? The problem is not that material is lacking on the subject. The word *glory* is found 194 times in the Old Testament and 161 times in the New Testament, not counting the many additional occurrences of the verb *to glorify*. However, books devoted exclusively to God's glory are scarce, and even standard theologies say little about it except in a general way or in a reference to church creeds. Just for fun I looked at the indexes in eight theologies. Only two include an entry for the "glory of God." Six (including my own!) had nothing.

Some years ago I listened to a series of messages on the glory of God. Though thoroughly biblical and well prepared, the series made only a slight impression on me. I remembered little of what was said. Why? Possibly because the speaker tried to include too many Scripture references without arranging them into categories that could be easily remembered. Nevertheless a seed had been planted, though in my own thinking a void remained.

Then, a few years ago I received an overseas phone call asking me to fill in at a Bible conference for another speaker who had to cancel. I said I would, and asked the director, Joe Jordan, if he had a theme in mind. "Yes," he replied, "the glory of God." I swallowed hard, because the conference was only a few weeks away, and I would need to prepare eight brand-new messages.

I studied. The Lord helped. The messages were prepared, given in English, interpreted into another language, and blessed by the grace of God.

In the few years since that conference, the subject has had time to mature and develop in my thinking to the point where I thought a book on the glory of God might help others. So I worked away at this book, revising those spoken messages and adding other ideas and chapters which came out of further study.

I think the most difficult task about putting this book together was deciding how to systematize the material to make it manageable for you the reader. As you will see, I decided simply to move through the Scriptures, emphasizing important areas concerning the glory of God in the Old and New Testaments.

Can a book on a subject like this be practical? Of course, if for no other reason than that it is biblically based, and we know that all Scripture is profitable for equipping us for every good work (2 Timothy 3:17). But the material became more obviously and personally practical as I wrote chapter after chapter. I hope you will find it so too.

Before sending the manuscript to the publisher, I asked four friends to read it. I am indebted to Paul Hook, Rick and Melanie Whittlesey, and Ed Yates for their suggestions—some humorous, some embarrassing to me, some difficult to accept (authors tend to think that what they write is infallible), but all helpful. My thanks too to my friends at Victor Books—Mark Sweeney and Wes Willis, whose friendships over many years have been very special, and Greg Clouse who has carefully edited my two most recent manuscripts.

Some of my books have a dedication; some do not. But the subject of this book requires a dedication, and there is only one that will do:

To Him who loves us,
and freed us from our sins
by His blood,
and has made us to be
a kingdom and priests
to serve His God and Father—
to Him be glory and dominion
forever and ever.
Amen.

Revelation 1:5-6

TRANSFORMED BY HIS GLORY

Chapter One

SHOW-OFF

Not to us, O Lord, not to us,
but to Your Name be the glory.

Psalm 115:1a

THE SCORE WAS 62–61 – OUR FAVOR.

With only seconds to play, we had the ball.

"Slow it down," yelled the coach from the sideline.

But suddenly, Tom, who had the ball, shot – and missed.

The opposing team rebounded the ball, quickly moved it down the court, and scored the winning basket.

We lost.

"Why?" I asked the coach afterward. "Why in the world did Tom shoot?"

"Oh," he replied, "the answer is simple. His girlfriend was in the stands, and he wanted to show off in front of her. He was trying to be a glory hog."

But, of course, instead of bringing joy and glory to himself and his college, he brought sorrow and shame.

In fact, the term *show-off* implies boasting, self-glory, pride, or that which is insincere and unworthy. Real glory implies just the opposite.

Now, if something or someone could be worthily and sincerely shown or seen without showing off, that would be pure, unadulterated glory. For that's what glory is – it is commendation or praise of someone or something because of seeing the sterling characteristics of that person or thing.

The Biblical Idea in the Old Testament

The principal Old Testament word for glory has the idea of being heavy, important, even awesome. "That's heavy, man," used to be a popular phrase with young people. So was the expression, "Awesome." Those popular sayings express quite well the meaning of the Old Testament word for glory.

The Old Testament uses the word to describe people who have wealth or importance. For example, Joseph told his brothers, "You must tell my father of all my splendor in Egypt and all that you have seen," referring to the position and wealth he had attained there (Genesis 45:13). The priestly garments made for Aaron were "for glory and for beauty" (Exodus 28:2). When David made plans for the temple which Solomon his son would build, he determined that it would be a place that would be "famous and glorious" (1 Chronicles 22:5). Such examples underscore the concept that glory relates to the intrinsic worth and splendor of the person or thing.

But that worth and splendor can be a source of pride and self-glory. In the time of Esther, for instance, Haman boasted to his wife and friends of the glory of his wealth and position in Xerxes' kingdom. He was an important man with awesome power. But his glory consisted of nothing more than showing off things about himself. His glory reeked with boastful pride (Esther 5:11).

The glory of God means the awesomeness, splendor, and importance of God seen in some way. When God is glorified, He is seen or shown in a pure, worthy, and sincere way. With God there can be no showing off with a sense of pride, for His character is perfect, and when He is seen, there is no mixture of wrong motives or sin. When, for example, Isaiah saw the glory of God, it was inseparably linked with the holiness of God: "Holy, holy, holy, is the Lord of hosts, the whole earth is full of His glory" (Isaiah 6:3). With God holiness and glory fit together in total compatibility. With us glory gets tinged with wrong, even sinful, motives.

The Biblical Idea in the New Testament

The New Testament word for glory comes from a word that means "to seem or think." Glory concerns what people think about something or someone, and thus refers to the reputation the person or object has. The glory of God is what He seems to be, which in His case is what He really is. It is God seen in some or all of His characteristics.

The New Testament word is also used in ways which include Old Testament ideas of glory. The glory of the Lord dazzled the shepherds at the announcement of the birth of Christ (Luke 2:9). Overpowering splendor characterized that scene. The Lord compared the glory of Solomon with the lilies of the field—and Solomon came out second best! (Matthew 6:28-29) A woman's long hair is said to be her glory (1 Corinthians 11:15). And the converts we win and nurture are our glory and joy (1 Thessalonians 2:19-20).

God has a number of facets to His character, and His glory may be seen sometimes through one facet and sometimes through another. But whenever even one of the aspects of His being is seen, He is glorified.

Prayers We Sometimes Pray

- Lord, glorify Yourself through this worship service.
- Lord, I want to glorify You in this step I am taking.
- Lord, here are our plans. Now be glorified through them.

What do we mean when we pray like this? Sometimes we mean for God to do anything that He wants in order to glorify Himself. In such prayers we do honestly give Him, so to speak, a blank check, and our motives are as pure as they can be.

But sometimes we seem to say that if God is glorified, success will be the inevitable result. The service will be used to bring people to Christ. My life will move from one victory to another. Our plans are the best possible, so get behind them, God, so that we can glorify You.

Suppose the service was an apparent flop. No response. Does that mean God was not glorified? Not necessarily.

19

Suppose someone lives the Christian life in obscurity. Or perhaps he or she constantly battles sin and temptation, seemingly without offering much spiritual benefit to the world. Does that mean God was not glorified? Not necessarily.

Suppose our plans have to be scrapped. Suppose the money does not come in the amount that was required to carry them to completion. Was God defeated? Not necessarily.

Perhaps His long-suffering and grace were shown in the service that seemed to flop. Perhaps His strength was made perfect in the weakness of what appeared to be an unsuccessful life. Perhaps His wisdom was demonstrated in the plans that needed to be scrapped or revised. If so, then God was glorified, even though not in the ways we expected when we prayed.

Our understanding or assumptions as to what glorifies God may be skewed or even totally wrong. Even our sincere prayers may be misguided ones. Too often we ask for God to be seen in ways that please us. When this happens, our showing off gets involved, the sight of Him becomes clouded, and His glory is obscured. James put it this way: "You ask and do not receive, because you ask with wrong motives [literally, evilly] so that you may spend it on your own pleasures" (James 4:3). *Spend* means "to squander," and from the Greek word for *pleasure* we derive our English word *hedonism*. No glory comes to God when we pray so as to squander the answers, should they come, on our hedonistic pleasures. And such pleasures need not be thought of only in terms of material things, but also in terms of intangible things, like self-promotion and self-glory.

This book will provide the opportunity to study some of the occasions and means God has used and continues to use to reveal His character and thus His glory. Although God's glory is something He possesses inherently, Scripture repeatedly emphasizes the revelation of His glory. Some of these manifestations we shall study, and in so doing we *should* see Him in His glory. And as we gaze on Him, our hearts can respond in worship and our lives in being those men and women who will reflect His glory.

Let God be seen. Let Him be seen in circumstances, in things, and in us. Then He will be truly glorified.

I am the Lord; that is My Name;
and I will not give My glory to another,
nor My praise to carved images.

Isaiah 42:8

Little children,
keep yourselves from idols.

1 John 5:21

Chapter Two

HOW TO SEE THE GLORY OF GOD AND LIVE TO TELL ABOUT IT

Satisfy us in the morning
with Your loving-kindness,
that we may sing for joy,
and be glad all our days.

Psalm 90:14,
a prayer of Moses
the man of God

was anxious to hear (2 Corinthians 2:12-13).

(2) Be careful if you decide to use a fleece either to try to determine the Lord's will or to confirm what you think it is. Gideon used a fleece (shorn wool) to confirm God's promise to deliver Israel through him. God had already announced that He would do so, but Gideon wanted confirmation (Judges 6:36-40). People sometimes use "fleeces" today to confirm or determine God's will. They will say, for instance, that if God does such-and-such then they can be sure that a course of action is the right one. Or, conversely, if God does not do something, then they will know what His will is for them. Putting out the fleece limits God to two options, and only the two the person thought of. God might have other options which we may not have even considered.

(3) Beware of self-generated "faith" to try to get the pillar to move. It would be unthinkable to imagine that Moses ever said to God, "I believe You want us to move in such-and-such direction. Now I will get the elders of Israel together and we will pray, believing that the pillar will move that way." Faith does not create something; rather, it is the avenue or channel through which the already existing promises of God come to us. God had promised Moses that His presence would go with the people. No amount of faith could create God's presence or the promise of His presence, nor could it move the pillar. Moses and the people exhibited their faith when they followed the pillar. Faith cannot force something to happen. Faith follows the promises of God which have been given to us in His Word.

In discerning God's will we should also be alert to these items:

(1) Always be aiming for Christlikeness. God leads us in paths of righteousness, never in paths of unrighteousness (Psalm 23:3). It is always important to ask, "What would Christ do in this situation?" Answering that question may not always give conclusive direction, but it may well eliminate some of the options.

41

(2) Think carefully about the ramifications of a decision. See if you can forecast what results a decision might bring several years later or what it might mean to other people.

(3) Seek advice from spiritually mature people, and people who know you, not from strangers who might tell you what you want to hear. "A wise man is he who listens to counsel" (Proverbs 12:15).

(4) Know the Scriptures as well as possible so that their general sense may guide you in those areas in which the Scriptures do not speak specifically.

(5) Be absolutely sure that you are willing to do anything God may want. Too often we impose our limited desires and our subjective feelings on Him and thus miss His will for us.

The glory of God is the manifestation of His character. God is surely seen when His will is done. So in a true sense the glory of God is doing the will of God. Let's always seek to do His will so that others may see His glory (Romans 12:1-2; 1 Corinthians 10:31).

Trust in the Lord with all your heart,
And do not lean on your own understanding.
In all your ways acknowledge Him,
And He will make your paths straight.

                                              Proverbs 3:5-6

Chapter Four

THE GLORY OF GOD JUDGING AND BLESSING

Lift up your heads, O gates,
and be lifted up, O ancient doors,
that the King of glory may come in.
Who is this King of glory?
The Lord strong and mighty,
the Lord mighty in battle.

Psalm 24:7-8

ODDLY ENOUGH, THE GLORY OF GOD JUDGES AS WELL as blesses. But even this makes sense because the glory of God is "God manifest." We know that God Himself both blesses and judges, so we would expect that the glory of God (which is the character of God displayed) would do the same.

God commissioned Ezekiel, who was both prophet and priest, to bring a message of judgment and blessing to the exiles of Judah in Babylon. And Ezekiel's ministry was laced throughout with visions and reminders of the glory of God. Thus Ezekiel's prophecy serves as a classic example of the glory of God in judgment and in blessing.

Three Waves of Deportation

The history of Israel is not exactly one of unswerving loyalty to the God who chose the nation and by so doing distinguished it above all others on the earth. Defection, idolatry, and disobedience characterized the people in every era. It started with the making of a golden calf at the very time Moses was receiving the Law from God on Mount Sinai. It continued to the time when priests were leaders in sin, and the people were breaking the Sabbath and intermarrying with non-Jewish people, all of which required reform under the ministry of Nehemiah. In between came the ups and downs of the period of judges, the wicked and idolatrous leadership of many of Israel's kings, the Assyrian captivity of the northern tribes, and a little more than a hundred years later the Babylonian conquest and deportation of Judah. All the while God sent messages of warning to the people—which they usually ignored.

45

(1) At the battle of Carchemish in 605 B.C., Nebuchadnezzar defeated the armies of Egypt (Jeremiah 46:2), went on to Palestine, made King Jehoiakim a vassal, and took Daniel and other hostages to Babylon. But Jehoiakim, a poor learner, sided with Egypt (to no avail) despite Jeremiah's warnings (22:13-19), and died just before Nebuchadnezzar came against Jerusalem again in 597.

(2) As a result of this second invasion Nebuchadnezzar captured newly enthroned King Jehoiachin, took him to Babylon, and installed Zedekiah as replacement vassal in Jerusalem. The Babylonian forces looted the treasures of the palace and the temple, took these heirlooms to Babylon, and deported 10,000 people (all but the poorest) including Ezekiel (2 Kings 24:10-16).

(3) But even in exile the people of Judah did not believe that God would continue to judge them if they did not repent. But He did. And in 586 Nebuchadnezzar's armies for the third time besieged Jerusalem and devastated it (2 Kings 25:11-21). They burned every important building in the city, including the temple and the royal palace, and broke down large sections of the city wall so that Jerusalem could not be easily defended in the future (verses 8-12).

Ezekiel's Commission

Ezekiel's ministry began after the second invasion of Jerusalem when the prophet was taken captive into Babylon and it continued in that foreign land for twenty-two years. This places his ministry from 593–571 B.C., from the time Ezekiel was thirty until he reached the age of fifty-two (Ezekiel 1:1-2; 29:17).

First, God told Ezekiel to go and speak His words to the people whether they would listen or not (2:7). Judgment was the thrust of the message he was to speak. Second, since God knew that the people were stubborn, obstinate, and hardheaded, He gave Ezekiel a head harder than theirs (3:7-8). And third,

46

God appointed Ezekiel to be a watchman over the house of Israel, and as a watchman to warn the people of impending judgment (3:17-21). Whether they heeded or rejected the warning was their responsibility, but warning them was the watchman's responsibility.

Ezekiel's Vision of the Glory of God

Before he was commissioned Ezekiel saw the glory of God (Ezekiel 1:4-28) and after his commissioning he saw it again (3:23). These appearances of the glory of God assured Ezekiel that his commission was indeed from God.

The vision recorded in Ezekiel 1 came in 593 while Ezekiel was with other exiles by the River Chebar, a navigable canal of the Euphrates River. Although some interpretations of this vision have been obviously fanciful and are to be rejected, perhaps the most important caution in interpreting the vision is not to lose sight of the forest for the trees. That is, do not get lost in the details and miss the main point. And Ezekiel himself tells us the main point is that he saw God (1:1) and the glory of God (1:28), which are the same, for God's glory is God displayed. Furthermore, Ezekiel refers back to this vision in other places in the prophecy when he saw similar visions (8:2-4; 10:15-22; 43:2-4).

• *The Vision as a Whole* (1:4). Ezekiel saw a storm coming from the north and a great cloud flashing fire from a center of reflecting metal. It must have looked like a violent electrical storm.

• *The Four Living Creatures and Wheels* (1:5-21). Within this spectacular cloud Ezekiel saw four living beings who had the general appearance of men, although they also had faces of lions, bulls, and eagles (1:10). They also had wings. Later Ezekiel identified these creatures as cherubim (10:20). Cherubim are an order of angels concerned with guarding the holiness and glory of God. They stood guard over the tree of life to keep Adam and Eve from eating its fruit after they had sinned, thus mercifully

47

preventing them from living forever in their sinful condition (Genesis 3:24). A representation of cherubim covered and guarded the mercy seat of the ark where God met and spoke to Israel (Exodus 25:18-22). God was enthroned between the cherubim of the ark (2 Samuel 6:2; Psalms 80:1; 99:1; Isaiah 37:16). Here too in this vision the cherubim are closely connected to the presence and glory of God.

Beside each cherub was a high, awesome, whirling, sparkling wheel, full of eyes on its rim. Each wheel appeared to have another wheel in it which intersected at a right angle. The cherubim and the wheels moved together. Many suggest that the cherubim formed a throne-chariot on which the glory of God rode (notice Psalm 18:10 and 1 Chronicles 28:18 which call the place where God was enthroned "the chariot").

● *God on His Throne* (1:22-28). Next Ezekiel saw a firmament or expanse—not an empty space but something solid like the firmament God created on the second day which supported the waters that were above it (Genesis 1:6-7). It had the awesome appearance of sparkling crystal or ice. The movement of the wings of the cherubim sounded like the noise of rushing water and an army in battle.

Ezekiel then became aware of something resembling a throne above the expanse, the rich blue color of lapis lazuli. On the throne was a figure with the appearance of a man whose brightness was like burning fire and a rainbow. Lest anyone should question what Ezekiel saw, he said clearly that it was the glory of the Lord.

The Ramifications of This Vision

There are at least two ramifications of this vision. One appears as Ezekiel's ministry unfolds. The glory of God underscored his message of judgment (9:3-10), and the glory of God accompanied His later message of hope and restoration (43:2-5; 44:4).

Throughout his ministry, Ezekiel and his message were affirmed by the appearance of the glory of God.

Another ramification was more immediate (recorded in 1:28). Ezekiel fell on his face before the Lord. So did the Apostle John when he saw the vision of the risen Christ (Revelation 1:17). And so should we prostrate ourselves before Him, if not in posture, certainly in attitude of heart and life as we worship and walk with Him. He is the great and almighty God and we are but insignificant creatures to whom He gives worth and work as we seek to be like Him and do His will.

The Departure of God's Glory

Fourteen months after Ezekiel had his vision of the glory of God recorded in chapter one, he had another (8:1–11:25). In this one he was transported back to Jerusalem so that God could show him the terrible idolatry being practiced there and thus the reason for His impending judgment on that city (in 586). Why?

God's indictment was clear: Devastation would soon come and with it the departure of His glory because the sin of the people was "very, very great" and because Jerusalem was "full of perversion" (9:9). Of what sins were the people guilty?

(1) At the northern gate of the inner court of the temple Ezekiel saw an "idol of jealousy" (8:5). The specific idol is not identified, but it was one which provoked God to jealous anger. Perhaps it was the image of Asherah, a Canaanite goddess of fertility. King Manasseh had put an image of Asherah in the temple (2 Kings 21:7), though he later removed it (2 Chronicles 33:15). Still later the reformer Josiah removed an Asherah pole from the temple and burned it (2 Kings 23:6). Perhaps another godless king had restored the burned idol to prominence, in direct violation of the second of the Ten Commandments (Exodus 20:4). What an affront to God!

(2) Next, Ezekiel was shown a place in the inner court of the

temple where the leaders of the nation were burning incense as they worshiped carvings of detestable animals and creeping things (Ezekiel 8:8-12).

This incident furnishes a great example of how actions are always related to theology—or, to put it in the vernacular, how what I do grows out of what I believe. The theology of these seventy leaders was defective in two areas. First, they apparently thought God could not know what they were doing because they did it in secret and in the dark (verse 12). But, of course, God is not hampered by closed doors or darkness, and He knew very well what was going on.

Let me illustrate. For one school year I was drafted to serve as dean of men in a Christian college. But even though almost all the students were Christians, they still had sin natures and youthful escapades. I used to tell some of the ringleaders to remember that even though I could not be everywhere at the same time or be awake all the time, God was, and that He saw just as clearly what they were doing at night when I had gone to bed as He did in the daytime when I was on duty. Years later, one of those fellows told me how much that remark got under his skin and reined him in—at least somewhat. But the leaders of Israel had forgotten that important bit of theology.

They also thought that since there had already been two invasions of Jerusalem God had deserted them (8:12; 9:9). Therefore they needed to seek help from the false gods represented by the idols they were worshiping. Their theology did not include the doctrine that God shows His love by punishing His people. Of course, they did not have Hebrews 12:5-11 in their Scriptures, but we do. Therefore, we must never conclude that God has abandoned us just because times are tough and difficulties abound in our lives. Such thinking reflects faulty theology.

(3) Some of the women were weeping for Tammuz, the god of vegetation and fertility (8:14). Since this vision occurred in August, possibly these women were trying to arouse Tammuz,

hoping he would bring springlike conditions to the earth out of season!

(4) In the inner court of the temple (where only priests were allowed) Ezekiel saw twenty-five men worshiping the sun (distinctly forbidden in Deuteronomy 4:19). Significantly, their backs were turned on the temple where true worship should have occurred (Ezekiel 8:16).

Clearly these sins show that the leaders and priests of the nation had exchanged the worship of the Creator for the worship of creatures (Romans 1:23-25), thus making God's indictment incontrovertible and His judgment inevitable.

The Apostle John warned believers to keep themselves from idols (1 John 5:21). Compromise or worldly perspective can lead even today to idolatry which God hates just as much as He did in Ezekiel's day.

The Stages of the Glory as It Departed

First, the glory of God arose from above the cherubim in the holy of holies and moved to the threshold of the temple (Ezekiel 9:3). Then it moved from there to the east gate of the temple (10:18-19). Finally, it left the city of Jerusalem and stood over the hill to the east of the city, the Mount of Olives (11:23).

At that point the vision ended; Ezekiel found himself again in Babylon; and he related all that he had seen to the exiles there.

The devastations which Jerusalem had suffered from the armies of Nebuchadnezzar were horrible enough, but God's removing His glory (His presence) from His temple, His priests, His leaders, His people, His city was more so.

Would God ever do a similar thing today? I think so. We know that the risen Christ threatened to remove the lampstand, that is, the church at Ephesus (Revelation 2:5). This threat likely did not mean He would close the doors, so to speak, but that His presence (glory) would no longer be in that church. Undoubtedly services would go on and activities even multiply, but without His presence in the group. And have not some churches done this, substituting programs for power and pep for purity? What a tragedy, but it does happen.

God's Glory Returning

Back to our prophet, Ezekiel, for the departure of God's glory does not end the story. In 573 God gave Ezekiel another vision, again taking him back to Jerusalem. Only by that time the third invasion and deportation had taken place (in 586). But now God gave him a vision of another temple to be built in the future millennial kingdom. It will be larger than Solomon's temple and thus also larger than Zerubbabel's (Haggai 2:3). Although this future temple and the renewal and restoration of Israel are described in great detail (Ezekiel 40–48), the return of the glory of God is central to the restoration. And return the glory will, from the east and into the temple to fill it with the presence of God (43:2-4; 44:4). This is God's promise, and when our Lord returns it will be totally fulfilled.

Because the Holy Spirit lives within all believers today (1 Corinthians 6:19), and because He securely seals us until we arrive in heaven (Ephesians 4:30), God will not withdraw His presence from our lives. To do this would mean that He would have to cause the Holy Spirit to leave us and break the seal with which He secured us. But too many Christians live lives that for all practical purposes exclude His presence and are therefore glory-less. For such people God is a convenience to be used when necessary, but not the control to be submitted to always. They want God to be a solver of problems, not a sustainer in the midst of them. And in their minds, love can only mean that God will cuddle us, never chasten us.

But His glory will return as we clean out the temple of our lives.

To Sum Up

The glory of God cuts both ways: to judge when we sin and come short of His glory (Romans 3:23), and to bless when we do all to His glory (1 Corinthians 10:31).

What? Do you not know that your body
is the temple of the Holy Spirit
who is in you, whom you have of God,
and you are not your own?
For you are bought with a price;
therefore, glorify God in your body.

1 Corinthians 6:19

Let the glory of the Lord endure forever.

Psalm 104:31

Chapter Five
THE POWER AND THE GLORY

From the rising of the sun
to the going down of the same,
the name of the Lord is to be praised.
The Lord is high above all nations,
and His glory above the heavens.

Psalm 113:3-4

BOTH THE OLD AND NEW TESTAMENTS RECORD THE revelation of the power and the glory of God in the world around us. Here is another way in which the glory of God is seen.

If the glory of God is God displayed by any or all of His attributes, certainly the world which surrounds us clearly displays His glory in several important ways.

The Glory of God Seen in His Power to Create

According to Jeremiah several of God's attributes reveal His glory in His work of creating the world. Three are specifically mentioned (power, wisdom, and understanding) when the prophet recorded the sharp contrast between the false gods of this world and the true God of this universe: "The gods that did not make the heavens and the earth shall perish from the earth and from under the heavens. It is He who made the earth by His power, who established the world by His wisdom; and by His understanding He has stretched out the heavens" (Jeremiah 10:11-12). The same prophet reiterated that God's power created the heavens and earth: "Ah Lord God! Behold, Thou has made the heavens and the earth by Thy great power and by Thine outstretched arm!" (32:17).

But unquestionably the principal Old Testament passage that details the glory of God in creation is Psalm 19:1-6. In these verses David answers several questions about the glory of God.

First, where do we see God's glory? (verse 1) We see it in the heavens; that is, in the expanse or firmament in the skies above us. This is the same word as used in the account of Creation in Genesis 1:6 and also refers to the heavens above us.

We can see about 3,000 stars when we look into the heavens with our eyes. Yet the Milky Way alone contains some 200 billion stars, and a million other galaxies exist in addition to the Milky Way. God put them all there and He keeps them in their respective places by His power.

However, the popular view today says that God did not do this, that it all evolved through natural processes and forces with no outside interference or help from any kind of divine being. The evolutionary view glorifies the power of nature in contrast to the biblical view that glorifies the power of God.

The second question David answers in this psalm is this: How often is the power and glory of God displayed in creation? (verses 1-2) Answer: Always. The tenses of the verbs in verses 1 and 2 indicate that the heavens continually tell of the glory of God and the work of His hands. Verse 2 says literally that the day bubbles forth speech from day to day, and the night reveals God's knowledge from night to night. There is never any time when mankind cannot be aware, if he will, of the glory of God in the creation that surrounds him.

Third question: How clear is this revelation of the glory of God? (verse 3) Answer: This revelation, though mute, is perfectly clear. Verse 3 plainly states that the revelation of God's glory is without words; it is nonverbal. Do not think, however, that something nonverbal or mute must be muffled or unclear. Not so. Think of common nonverbal ways we all use at times to communicate. A frown. A smile. Hands on hips. A wink of the eye. A clenched fist. An aggressive stance. Indeed, nonverbal communication can be even clearer than verbal communication. Likewise the heavens communicate clearly, though without words, the power and wisdom of God, thus revealing these aspects of His glory.

Fourth, how widespread is this revelation? (verse 4) Answer: It is universal or worldwide. *Their line* means "their call"; that is, the call of the heavens to acknowledge the glory of God goes to the entire world. What a vivid picture! The heavens above are calling to people everywhere to look up and acknowledge that God exists. Tragically, millions of people never hear (or see) the call and live their lives as if there were no God. And some Christians do too.

Fifth, how strong is this revelation? (verses 4b-6) Answer: As strong as the sun. In the heavens God has placed the sun which is likened here to a bridegroom about to be married or an athlete about to run a race. The sun runs its course throughout all the world and nothing can be hidden from its heat. Even a blind person who cannot see the stars or the clouds can feel the warmth of the sun. And because he can, he should ask himself where that heat is coming from. The sun is a strong nonverbal message that a powerful and wise God exists who created this world.

The name of God used in this section of the psalm is, most appropriately, *El.* The name denotes power, leadership, authority, and greatness. Furthermore, *Elohim* (from the root El) is the name of God used forty-six times in the account of Creation in Genesis 1–2. Creation demonstrates God's power, leadership, authority, and greatness, and all of those characteristics reveal His glory.

The principal New Testament passage concerning the glory of God as seen in His power to create is Romans 1:18-20. In these verses Paul charges that God's wrath is revealed against all who suppress truth and practice ungodliness. The reason for this wrath is that instead of acknowledging what can be known of God from creation, mankind rejected that knowledge and, indeed, perverted it. What has been made, namely, the world, clearly reveals (and has since the beginning of Creation) God's power and divine nature. In other words, all mankind should know from observing the universe around him that a supreme Being exists. But instead, mankind rejects that truth and makes idols for himself, simply because man can be supreme over idols rather than acknowledging a God who is supreme over him.

Creation does not reveal *everything* about God, but, according to Romans 1:20, it reveals His power and divine nature. Perhaps these two ideas—power and divine nature—can be merged to say that creation clearly demonstrates that there exists in this universe a powerful supreme Being. And adding what is revealed about God in Psalm 19:1-6 we can conclude that creation shows God's glory through His attributes of power, intelligence, and supreme divinity.

The Glory of God Seen in His Power to Sustain the Universe

Paul writes in Colossians 1:16-17: "For by Him all things were created, both in the heavens and on earth, visible and invisible, whether thrones or dominions or rulers or authorities—all things have been created by Him and for Him. And He is before all things, and in Him all things hold together." Here Creation is said to be the work of Christ (as also in John 1:3 and Hebrews 1:3). Such a statement does not surprise us since Christ is God. But an additional fact is revealed also—in Him all things hold together. The Greek word for "hold together" occurs only here in the New Testament. It means that all things cohere or are bonded together in Christ. He keeps everything in this universe in order and sustains all things.

If, for example, Christ were not keeping all things in order, there could be no successful space program. A vehicle would be launched or a probe to a distant planet sent aloft, but if Christ were not keeping all things in order there would be no guarantee that the planet would be in the anticipated place when the probe arrived. Men could not have landed on the moon if scientists could not have been assured that the moon would be where they thought it should be when they launched the spacecraft. Can you imagine the confusion and consternation that

could not understand and fully grasp the answer simply because we do not see the end from the beginning nor can we even begin to imagine how all the pieces of His plan fit together. But fit they do, and it is the power of the word of Christ who is the radiance (not reflection) of God's glory that accomplishes it all.

The universe constantly shows us the glory of God in three ways: (1) in the creation of the universe by God's power which in turn displays not only His power but also His intelligence and His divine nature; (2) in the universe's being constantly sustained by the power of Christ; and (3) in its being moved in all of its events, circumstances, and opposition to the goals and ends for which God made the ages. Surely the power and the glory belong to God and our Lord Jesus Christ.

You are worthy, our Lord and our God,
to receive glory and honor and power;
for You have created all things,
and because of Your will,
they existed and were created.

Revelation 4:11

Chapter Six

THE GLORY
OF GOD
IN THE LIFE
OF OUR LORD

But I seek not My own glory.

John 8:50

THE LORD JESUS CHRIST DID NOT BEGIN TO EXIST AT the time of His incarnation. He, like the Father and the Holy Spirit, is eternal.

Nor did glory come upon Him when He was born in Bethlehem. He had glory along with the Father before the world began. Shortly before His death He prayed that His Father would glorify Him with "the glory which I had with You before the world was" (John 17:5).

Just as Moses could not look on the face of God and live, so mankind could not have looked on the unveiled glory of the Son of God when He lived here in this world. Nevertheless, people did see the glory of God revealed in Christ during His earthly life. "And the Word became flesh, and dwelt among us, and we beheld His glory, glory as of the only begotten from the Father, full of grace and truth" (John 1:14). When God showed Moses His glory, He showed him, among other things, His grace (Exodus 33:19; 34:6). When our Lord took on Himself humanity and was born into this world, He displayed, among other things, God's grace. John repeats this truth when he contrasts the Law which was given through Moses with grace and truth that came through Christ (John 1:17).

But we did not live during the earthly lifetime of our Lord. How can we see His glory? Two ways. First, when we were saved, God caused light to shine in our hearts—light which gives the knowledge of the glory of God in the face of Jesus Christ (2 Corinthians 4:6). When salvation floods our hearts we see the glory of it in the face of our Savior. In this verse Paul refers to God's creating light at the time of Creation as the prototype of that which God does whenever a soul accepts the

67

Savior. Each one experiences the light of the knowledge of the glory of God in the person of Christ. God is light (1 John 1:5), so whenever a person believes in Christ God enters that life to dispel its darkness. Paul uses the same verb (translated "shined" in 2 Corinthians 4:6) in Acts 26:13 (though compounded here) of his own conversion. That enlightenment, Paul goes on to say, consists in the knowledge of the glory of God. Just as Moses' face reflected the glory of God after he spoke to God face-to-face (Exodus 34:29-35), so we who have come to know the glory of God in the person of Christ can reflect it as well.

Second, we can see the glory of Jesus Christ as we read and study the written records of the earthly life of our Lord and see how the glory of God was revealed in Him. And this is what we shall summarize in this chapter.

As we study His life and glory we need to remember that we are to "follow in His steps" (1 Peter 2:21) and "to walk in the same manner as He walked" (1 John 2:6). Although both these passages emphasize the self-sacrificing love of our Lord, they also include other aspects of His life which we are to imitate. Of course, we can never in this life perfectly imitate Him, for He was without sin and we are not. But as we seek to follow the example of His earthly life, we too can glorify God in our bodies as we live in this world (1 Corinthians 6:20).

Ways Our Lord Glorified God in His Private Life

● *By knowing the Scriptures.* Christ did not learn the Scriptures by attending the rabbinical schools of His day—He learned them at home (John 7:15; Acts 4:13). The home in which our Lord was reared was a godly one. The Old Testament Scriptures were known and loved in it. His mother Mary's great burst of praise (known as the Magnificat, Luke 1:46-55) contains 15 discernible quotations from the Old Testament. The Book of James, written by our Lord's half brother, is divided into 108 verses in our English Bibles. In those 108 verses 22 Old Testament books are alluded to, again showing how much the Old Testament was known by the members of Christ's family.

When our Lord was tempted by Satan He was able to resist by quoting passages from Deuteronomy (8:3; 6:16; 6:13). When Satan quoted from Psalm 91 (Matthew 4:6), he omitted a phrase which was not suited to his purpose, and our Lord picked up on that. Satan left out part of verse 11 — "to guard you in all your ways." The omission distorts the meaning of the promise, which is that God will keep the righteous in their way, not that He will preserve them when they take needless risks. And a needless risk was exactly what Satan had proposed to our Lord. Our Lord not only knew the Scriptures in detail, but He obviously considered the details significant and trustworthy.

In addition, our Lord knew and used a number of the stories of the Old Testament as historically accurate. Notice the following:

(1) He verified that Adam and Eve were created by God as two individual human beings and that they were active in a truly historical situation (Matthew 19:3-5; Mark 10:6-8).

(2) He referred to the destruction of the city of Sodom and to the chief characters in that story, Lot and his wife (Matthew 10:15; 11:23; Luke 17:28-29).

(3) He referred to the events connected with the flood in Noah's day and used those events to describe conditions before His second coming (Matthew 24:37-39; Luke 17:26-27).

(4) He compared His own resurrection to the true story of Jonah and the great fish (Matthew 12:40).

(5) He referred to Isaiah (Matthew 12:17); Elijah (Matthew 17:11-12); Daniel (Matthew 24:15); Abel (Matthew 23:35); Zechariah (Matthew 23:35); Abiathar (Mark 2:26); David (Matthew 22:45); Moses and his writings (Matthew 8:4; John 5:46); Moses at the burning bush (Mark 12:26); and Abraham, Isaac, and Jacob (Matthew 8:11; John 8:39).

According to an extrabiblical source, Jesus' father Joseph died when He was a teenager. We know from Matthew 13:55-56 that there were at least seven children in the family, Jesus being the eldest. So when His father died, our Lord would have been the One on whom the burden of supporting the family would have fallen. The point of mentioning this is to remind us that He was busy with work and family responsibilities, yet He made time to learn the Scriptures.

To glorify God we must not only know what God is like but also what He likes. And the only way for us to know those things is to know His Word. Then we can glorify God all the more and also imitate our Lord.

• *By maintaining fellowship with His Father through prayer.* We have glimpses of our Lord praying on a number of occasions. The night before choosing the twelve disciples He went alone to the mountain and prayed all night (Luke 6:12). But He did not do that every night. In fact I daresay that He slept most nights. On one occasion He was praying before daybreak (Mark 1:35). But we do know that He prayed often (Luke 5:16). (See also Matthew 14:23; 19:13; Mark 14:32-39; Luke 3:21; 6:12-13; 9:18; 11:1; 22:32; John 11:41-42.)

"Christ's teaching on prayer is extensive and profound. Prayer should be continuous (Luke xviii. 1); private and public (Matt. vi. 6; Luke xviii. 10); reverent and familiar (Matt. vi. 6; John iv. 24); sincere and earnest (Matt. vi. 7; vii. 7); definite (Matt. vii. 7-11); missionary (Matt. ix. 38); believing (Matt. xvii. 20, 21); united (Matt. xviii. 19, 20); watchful (Matt. xxvi. 41)" (W. Graham Scroggie, *A Guide to the Gospels,* London: Pickering & Inglis, 1948, p. 566).

If He who is God needed to pray to His Father, certainly we do even more so.

• *By being committed to doing the will of God.* When our Lord was about to come to earth in the Incarnation it was said of Him that He came to do the will of God (Hebrews 10:7). During His

70

entire life He could say that He always did those things which were pleasing to the Father (John 8:29). And at the end of His earthly life He reaffirmed His commitment to do the will of His Father (Matthew 26:39). If we follow in His steps then we too must take the place of slaves who do all that our Master desires.

Our Lord Glorified God in His Public Life

This commitment to do the will of God was, of course, the basis for all the works our Lord did while on earth. And in many instances we are told that the people who observed Christ glorified God because of what He did in obeying the will of His Father.

For example, after our Lord healed and forgave the sins of the paralyzed man whose friends let him down through the roof of the house, the crowd who witnessed the healing was filled with awe and glorified God (Matthew 9:8; Mark 2:12; Luke 5:25-26). Again, when our Lord raised from death the only son of a widow at Nain, those who saw this were in awe and glorified God (Luke 7:16). And when on another occasion He healed many who were dumb or lame or blind, the people likewise glorified God (Matthew 15:31). Peter summarized our Lord's ministry by saying that He went about doing good and healing those who were oppressed by the devil (Acts 10:38).

In reading the Gospels one notices a number of things about our Lord's public ministry. He displayed compassion (Matthew 9:36; Mark 6:34). He loved people (Mark 10:21). He offered to help before He was asked (John 5:6). He faithfully attended the worship of God in the synagogue (Luke 4:16). He always did those things that pleased the Father and went about doing good. That glorifies God because God is good. We glorify God and we imitate our Savior when we do good works. "Let your light shine before men in such a way that they may see your good works, and glorify your Father who is in heaven" (Matthew 5:16).

Ways Our Lord Glorified God in the Priorities in His Life

None of us can do everything. Neither did our Lord. We need to have priorities, just as He did.

(1) He placed spiritual needs ahead of physical needs. Clearly our Lord did not heal everyone with whom He came in contact or who needed physical healing. In the recorded miracles of Christ which were performed on specific individuals or groups there are thirty-nine cases of healing. But He did not heal all those who needed it. For example, a multitude of sick, blind, lame, and withered were gathered at the pool of Bethesda (John 5:3), yet Christ threaded His way through the crowd to find a single individual to heal, a man who exhibited no faith that he could be healed. Our Lord could have healed others that day, but He did not. If need carries with it a responsibility to respond, then our Lord furnishes no example of this in His ministry of physical healing.

Neither did our Lord feed all who were hungry. On two occasions He fed over 10,000 people, but only a single meal. He did not continue to supply them with food, though some of them undoubtedly continued to have a genuine need for food.

These miracles were done to glorify God, or to teach the disciples, or to confirm the Lord's claim to be God. Thus the physical benefits were secondary to the spiritual lessons intended to be learned.

The angel's announcement to Joseph said that Christ would "save His people from their sins" (Matthew 1:21). John the Baptist designated Him as the "Lamb of God who takes away the sin of the world" (John 1:29). Of His own mission He said that He came "to seek and to save that which was lost" (Luke 19:10). True, He came to teach, to serve, to set an example, but above all, He came, as His primary purpose, to save. In every aspect of His life on earth, but most especially in His sacrificial death for our sins He glorified God (John 17:4).

(2) He placed serving others ahead of insisting on His own rights. One of the clearest examples of this principle is found in the incident concerning paying the temple tax (Matthew 17:24-27). This tax was based on the regulation of Exodus 30:11-16 and was collected annually from every male Jew twenty or over, including those living in foreign countries. The money was used to keep the temple in Jerusalem in good repair.

Seeking out Peter, the tax collectors asked him if Jesus would pay the tax. Peter responded quickly and affirmatively, but then had second thoughts. Anticipating Peter's misgivings, the Lord questioned Peter and instructed him in the uniqueness of His person. There followed a brief dialogue that led to the conclusion that Jesus, as the owner of the temple (because He is God, Malachi 3:1), was exempt from paying the tax. Nevertheless, through a miracle of finding a coin in a fish's mouth, the taxes for Peter and the Lord were paid.

However, it is the reason Christ paid that is so instructive of His priorities—"lest we give them offense" (Matthew 17:27). The same verb is used in Romans 14:21 and 1 Corinthians 8:13 to teach that Christians should sometimes surrender their freedom for the sake of others. Here the Lord demonstrated a principle all reformers could well follow; i.e., avoid actions that are not essential to the success of the mission. Not offending for the sake of His mission took priority over insisting on His own rights.

This lesson is frequently forgotten today among God's people. Believers too often say, "But I have the right . . ." and all too often finish that sentence this way: " . . . to be happy." Surely, they reason, God wants me to be happy, and therefore I have the right to do whatever makes me happy. As a believer I have a right to be a slave of righteousness (Romans 6:18). I have the right to give up my rights. I have the right to show God and His salvation to this world. I have the right to imitate my Lord and thus glorify God.

Anticipating His approaching death and resurrection our Lord said: "The hour has come for the Son of Man to be glorified" (John 12:23). Self-sacrificing love was at the center of His glory. So it should also be with us.

Therefore, be imitators of God, as dear children . . . walk in love . . . walk as children of light . . . walk carefully . . . be not foolish but understand what the will of the Lord is.

Ephesians 5:1, 2, 8, 15, 17

Chapter Seven

THE GLORY OF GOD IN THE NEW COVENANT

OR

IF YOU THINK MOSES HAD GLORY, LOOK WHAT WE HAVE

And the Word became flesh,
and tabernacled among us,
and we beheld His glory,
glory as of the only begotten
from the Father,
full of grace and truth.
For the Law was given through Moses;
grace and truth came
through Jesus Christ.

John 1:14, 17

---

but Jesus puts God's grace on display

UNDER THE OLD COVENANT, THAT IS, THE MOSAIC Law, the glory of the Lord was principally related to the tabernacle (Exodus 40:34). But, as we have studied, Moses also had a special encounter with the glory of the Lord (33:22) which resulted in a shining face every time he spoke with God. In fact his face shone so much that each time he came out to the people he had to put a veil over it (34:29-35).

Some Purposes of the Old Covenant

The Mosaic Law was holy (Romans 7:12) since it was given by a holy God to make His people a holy nation (Exodus 19:6). It contained, by Jewish count, 613 commandments that governed every aspect of the lives of the Jewish people. The Law told people how to live in a manner pleasing to God, but it could not save, for good works never can save. "By the works of the Law no flesh will be justified in His sight" (Romans 3:20). It could show a man his deficiencies and sins and point him to his need of the Messiah, but it of itself could not save (1 Timothy 1:8-10). On the other hand, the Law distinguished Israel and set the nation apart from all other nations on earth at that time.

When our Lord came to earth He was the outshining of God's glory (Hebrews 1:3). The word *outshining* or *brightness* or *radiance* indicates that He did not merely reflect God's glory; He shined it out from His person. And yet it must have been veiled; otherwise, no one could have dared to look at Him. By His death He established the New Covenant with His people, the church, and this is the covenant under which we who have believed now live (Luke 22:20; 2 Corinthians 3:6).

The Superiority of the New Covenant

Nowhere are the contrasts between the Old Covenant and the New Covenant more sharply distinguished and the superiority of the New displayed than in 2 Corinthians 3:6-16:

The Old	The New
Letter kills (verse 6)	Spirit gives life (verse 6)
Is a ministry of death (verse 7)	Is a ministry of the Spirit (verse 8)
Came with glory (verse 7)	Came with more glory (verse 8)
Had no glory (verse 10)	Surpassing glory (verse 10)
Has been done away with (verse 11)	Remains (verse 11)
Bred hiddenness (verse 13)	Breeds boldness (verse 12)
Hardens hearts (verse 14)	Saves hearts (verse 16)

These characteristics of the Old Covenant form a severe indictment against it and at the same time elevate the New to a most superior place in the economies of God. Who would daresay, for example, that the Mosaic Law ministers death? Who would charge that it hardens hearts? Who would level these accusations against the Mosaic Law, including the Ten Commandments? Paul did, for he expressly highlighted the part of the Law that was engraved on stones—the Ten Commandments. Of course, 9 of the Ten Commandments are included in the teachings of the New Covenant, so they become part of the superior covenant. But as part of the Old Covenant, they have been done away with, as have the other 613 commandments.

Some of the Glorious Provisions of the New Covenant

(1) *Transformation.* The New Covenant transforms us from glory to glory (2 Corinthians 3:17-18). Who transforms us? The

Lord Jesus and the Holy Spirit. "The Lord is the Spirit" (verse 17) is a strong statement that both are of the same essence and deity. Both Christ, who is God, and the Holy Spirit, who is God, are involved in our sanctification.

What is the basis for our ability to be transformed? It is the freedom of grace (in the New Covenant) as contrasted with the bondage of the Law (in the Old Covenant). So the basis or prerequisite for freeing us is the liberty which the Spirit of the Lord gives to us. From what does He free us?

• From bondage to the Law in relation to our sanctification. "For if you are led by the Spirit you are not under the Law" (Galatians 5:18).

• From the fear of slavery into the freedom of being adopted into the family of God (Romans 8:15).

• From the bondage of the old life and its sinful ways (Romans 7:6).

• And ultimately from all the corruption of this life into the freedom of the completion of our redemption and reception of, among other things, our new bodies (Romans 8:21, 23).

What does it mean to be transformed? This same word is sometimes translated transfigure. It is used in the account of our Lord's transformation on the Mount of Transfiguration (Matthew 17:2). Paul also uses it to describe the process of our sanctification. We are to be transformed or transfigured by the renewing of our minds (Romans 12:2). To be transformed means to be changed—changed into the image of Christ.

How does this happen? It occurs stage by stage as we behold the glory of the Lord. Not all at once, but little by little, increment by increment. It is a process, not a single event, and a process that lasts throughout our entire Christian life. Not only are Christ and the Holy Spirit involved, but we are too. For, Paul says, we behold the glory of the Lord as in a mirror and are then transformed. In other words we have to study the Lord in the Word—the mirror—and conform our lives to what we learn.

79

In this way we reflect His glory in our lives. But it takes effort to study and commitment to live. Sanctification normally is a cooperative effort involving both the Lord and us. Sometimes the Lord may be involved in a greater way than I am, and sometimes the reverse may be true. There is no common formula that says, for example, that God gives 50 percent of the effort and I give 50 percent. But normally sanctification combines both divine and human activity (Romans 8:13).

If, then, I am responsible to behold the glory of the Lord in order to be transfigured into His image, where do I see that glory? Principally in the written Word of God. True, I may behold the glory of the Lord as I hear what God has done for others, but the only totally, completely reliable place to learn about His glory is in the written Word. And this takes a lifelong and disciplined effort on my part. I cannot behold the glory of the Lord in a closed Bible. I cannot behold the glory of the Lord in a Bible I do not understand. I must read, study, and learn. To guide the entire effort I will need the teaching ministry of the Holy Spirit (John 16:13-15). Under the Old Covenant people did not have the full and complete revelation from God which includes the New Testament. They did not experience all the ministries of the Holy Spirit we do today under the New Covenant. So if you think Moses and the Israelites had it good, we have it far better. Let us use all the provisions God has given us under this superior New Covenant.

(2) *Good news.* The New Covenant gives us a Gospel of the glory of Christ (2 Corinthians 4:1-7). What is this good news about the glory of Christ? It is not just any good news, but a very specific one. It concerns the glory of Christ who is the image of God. Glory means to show, demonstrate. So the glory of Christ means showing who He is. And the Gospel of the glory of Christ means the good news about who our Lord is.

And who is He? He is the image of God, God Himself. He is Lord (verse 5) which means in this instance the resurrected

80

One. He is Christ; that is, the Messiah. He is Jesus; that is, the perfect human being. And because He is who He is, we have good news to announce to this needy, hurting world. Our Gospel would not be authentic if it did not have this Person to validate it.

When we believed in Christ, light shone into our hearts, and we were given the ministry of making that good news known to others (4:1, 6). And we should be constant and faithful in doing this. Paul gives some guidelines for witnessing concerning this good news (4:1-2):

• Never lose heart because of adverse circumstances, opposition, or lack of results.

• Never use underhanded practices.

• Never try to be crafty. This word *crafty* is the same word used later by Paul to describe how Satan deceived Eve in the Garden of Eden (2 Corinthians 11:3).

• Never adulterate the Word of God by falsifying it or by trying to make it acceptable, rather than letting it speak as it was written. Just tell the message about the wonderful person of Christ clearly and simply. That is what we are privileged to do. And as people believe they too receive the knowledge of the glory of God in the face of Jesus Christ.

(3) *Ministry.* The New Covenant gives us a ministry for which others will thank God and in so doing glorify Him (2 Corinthians 4:8-15). The key verse is verse 15: "For all things are for your sakes, that the grace which is spreading to more and more people may cause the giving of thanks to abound to the glory of God." Paul's consuming goal in life was to minister so that God might be glorified. And he did this in the midst of very difficult circumstances. Notice what he wrote in verses 8-10. He was afflicted. That word means hard-pressed, hemmed-in. He was perplexed or despairing, though not completely. He was persecuted almost constantly as he went from place to place. He was struck down, perhaps a reference to being stoned at Lystra

81

(Acts 14:19). He was always exposed to death—like our Lord—so that others might live.

This does not paint the picture of "success" according to our contemporary ideas of the term. But it does paint the portrait of a servant who does not let outward circumstances detract or sidetrack him. Joy in Christ does not depend on favorable and comfortable circumstances. Joy comes:

- When God answers prayer (John 16:24)
- When we keep His commandments (John 15:10-11)
- When we hear of the conversions of others (Acts 15:3; 1 Thessalonians 2:19-20)
- Whenever the Gospel of Jesus Christ is preached regardless of the good or bad motives of those who preach it (Philippians 1:17-18)
- When we see others whom we have helped progressing in the Christian life (Philippians 2:2; 1 Thessalonians 3:9; 2 John 4; 3 John 4)
- And above all, as we rejoice in the Lord always (Philippians 4:4).

If our circumstances in life are pleasant, we thank God and use them for His glory (1 Timothy 2:2). If not, we still rejoice in Him and do not consider adversity to be an unusual experience for the people of God (Romans 8:36).

How do I glorify God under the New Covenant? I glorify Him when the light of the Gospel shines in my heart. I glorify Him as I move from stage to stage in Christian growth. I glorify Him as I spread the message to others. I glorify Him as others thank God for my ministry. All of these actions and activities glorify God simply because they show others more and more of who God is. And all of this is possible because God has given us a New Covenant that replaces the Old.

(4) *Future glory.* The New Covenant gives us the promise of future glory (2 Corinthians 4:16-18). In 2 Corinthians 1:8 Paul says that his afflictions were life threatening. That's how severe

they were. And yet he says that they were momentary, light, and not disheartening (4:16-17). How can he say that? Was he trying to kid himself? Not at all. He simply placed his afflictions in comparison with what awaits all Christians in the future. And that is an eternal weight of glory. Our circumstances may overwhelm us to the point of despairing of life itself. Yet these are temporary and light burdens when compared with the eternal weight of glory which will be ours to carry about. Someone once said we will need to have glorified bodies to be able to carry that weight of glory. The person may not have been totally serious when he said that, but I rather like that suggestion. Our present bodies are weighed down with all kinds of problems, but someday we will have a body that can bear the glorious and eternal weight of glory.

Imagine a pair of scales, the kind where you put the things to be weighed on one side and the weights on the other side. Put all the problems of this life on the one side, and on the other place the eternal weight of glory. No matter how much adversity or how many problems you place on the one side, the scales will immediately go "plunk" as they give way to the weight of glory. All of the things of this life cannot and will not move the scales at all.

Moses Versus Us

Moses had it good. We have it far better. He had the Old Covenant. We have the New Covenant. (1) We have a new means of sanctification by the indwelling Christ and Spirit who move us from glory to glory. (2) We have a new message which brings the light of the knowledge of the glory of God in Christ to all who believe. (3) We have a ministry which spreads that message to others who also will bring glory to God. (4) And we have a hope that someday we will have eternal glory. In the meantime and for all our days and years, let's serve to His glory.

Whoever speaks, let him speak, as it were, the utterances of God; whoever serves, let him do so as by the strength which God supplies; so that in all things God may be glorified through Jesus Christ, to whom belongs the glory and dominion forever and ever. Amen.

1 Peter 4:11

Chapter Eight

THE GLORY OF GOD IN THE CHURCH

O, the depth of the riches both of the wisdom
and knowledge of God!
How unsearchable are His judgments
and unfathomable His ways!
For who has known the mind of the Lord,
or who became His counselor?
Or who has first given to Him
that it might be paid back to Him again?
For from Him and through Him and to Him
are all things.
To Him be the glory forever. Amen.

Romans 11:33-36

HOW DOES GOD'S GLORY SHOW ITSELF IN THE CHURCH? Before we answer that question, let's walk through a brief but significant word study. The basic Greek word *perisseuo* means "to abound or exceed." The Lord used it in the Sermon on the Mount (Matthew 5:20) to say that entrance into God's kingdom demands righteousness that "exceeds" that of the scribes and Pharisees. Now sincere Pharisees did try to live righteous lives. They knew the Scriptures (Matthew 23:2); they tithed (Luke 18:12); they fasted twice a week (Matthew 9:14; Luke 18:12); they were diligent in prayer (Mark 12:40; Luke 18:10); and they tried to obey the Mosaic Law (Mark 2:24). Actually some succeeded (Philippians 3:6), for some were zealous for their beliefs and tried to live them (Acts 26:10-11). To exceed that lifestyle, as Christ commanded, was no small thing.

The Lord used the same word in the Parable of the Prodigal Son. When the young man came to his senses in the far country he remembered that in his father's house the servants had "more than enough bread" (NASB), "food to spare" (NIV), "bread enough and to spare" (KJV)—Luke 15:17. The translators seem to struggle to express the expansiveness of this word, but all agree that it means "more than enough."

Paul used this same basic word to describe the "abundance" of the liberality of the churches in Greece with respect to the collection he was gathering for the poor believers in Palestine (2 Corinthians 8:2). Again, the basic word conveys much abundance.

In the language of the New Testament the meaning of a word may be intensified by adding a prepositional prefix to it. So is the case with this word we have been studying. The base word with a prefix appears in Romans 5:20: "Where sin abounded, grace did much more abound." "More abound" is the basic word *abound* with a prepositional prefix (*huperperisseuo*). In other words, the superabundant grace of God takes away all our sin.

Why I Failed an Assignment

We do this sort of intensifying in English by using an adverb after the verb. Let me illustrate. I do not remember many specifics about the first few years of my schooling. I must have learned to read and write, among other things. But I do remember quite vividly one incident from one of those very early grades. It would most likely have been a Monday morning class because the teacher had asked each of us to draw a picture of something that occurred over the previous weekend and then give the picture a title.

It so happened that I had seen a house on fire during the weekend. In fact it had completely burned. I have no idea now whether or not that was the first time I had seen such a fire, but likely so. In any case it impressed me greatly. So I drew my crude little picture of a house, and then I drew tongues of fire licking up its sides, and then I gave it a title: "The House That Burned Up." I guess it was by instinct that I added the word *up*, but I wanted to convey the idea that this was not a fire confined to a single room or area of the house but rather one that consumed the entire structure. So I said it had burned up, not just that it had burned.

The teacher said, "That's wrong. The title should have been 'The House That Burned Down.' " Now I really do not know if houses burn up or down, just as I am not sure whether someone who eagerly consumes a meal gobbles his food up or gobbles it down. But in both cases the adverb after the verb intensifies the meaning of the verb. In New Testament Greek a prefix on the verb has the same effect.

Super-superabundant

Now consider the basic word *perisseuo* compounded with two prepositions *(huperekperisseuo)*. How should it be translated to convey the doubly intensified idea of abounding? It is so used in Ephesians 3:20: "Unto Him who is able to do exceeding abundantly above all that we ask or think" (KJV); or "immeasurably more" (NIV); or how about super-superabundantly? God is able to do super-superabundantly above all things, and certainly above what we can ask or think. The expansiveness, depth, and abundance in the doubly compounded form of the basic word (which of itself conveys a large concept) is almost beyond our comprehension.

Ephesians 3:20-21 appears in this place in Paul's letter not only as a prayer promise but also, if not primarily, as a doxology. Paul ascribes glory to God in the church and in Christ Jesus for some very major things He has done. These verses do not constitute a promise that we can ask anything we want or think about and expect answers. They ascribe glory to God for what He has done in the church and in Christ.

How God Glorifies Himself in the Church

How is God glorified by the use of His super-superabundant power? God is glorified by bringing Jews and Gentiles together in the one body of Christ—the one new man—through the blood of Christ (Ephesians 2:13-16). Living, as we do, almost 2,000 years after this event took place, most of us probably cannot appreciate how great a change and accomplishment this was. But notice the way Paul describes the position of the Gentiles before the body of Christ began. We were "without Christ," "aliens from the commonwealth of Israel," "strangers from the covenants of promise," "no hope," "without God," "far off," at "enmity," "strangers," "foreigners" (Ephesians 2:12-15). But now, by the super-superabundant power of God, believing Gentiles along with believing Jews have been joined not to Judaism or even a redesigned Judaism but to form "a new man," to be placed together in the household of God, to become a building which the Holy Spirit inhabits. None of this could have been accomplished except by the super-superabundant power of God.

How We Glorify God in the Church

Creating the new man, the body of Christ, is something only God could do. But in the verses preceding this doxology Paul does mention four things he prayed about which could only have been answered by the super-superabundant power of God. These are not "small" petitions, and they are appropriate to most, if not all, believers.

(1) *Not becoming disheartened.* Paul asks that the believers not be disheartened by the troubles he was experiencing (Ephesians 4:13). Actually, he says, they are for "your glory." What troubles? Paul was in Rome under house arrest awaiting the disposition of his case before Caesar. He had been there two years (Acts 28:30). Roman law gave the accusers of someone on trial before Caesar eighteen months to appear and present their case. If they did not show up in that amount of time, then the case was automatically decided in favor of the accused. Apparently Paul's accusers decided not to press their case (probably realizing that they would not win it). So they simply let the eighteen months (plus the few extra months Paul was in Rome before and afterward) pass. This accomplished two things. Paul was kept out of circulation, and somewhat of a cloud was left over him which would not have been there had Caesar announced a verdict of not guilty and thus vindicated him.

To have two years taken out of one's life and to be confined for most of it would be tough for anybody. But to be removed from public and itinerant ministry would be especially hard on someone like Paul. What's more, some took advantage of Paul's confinement to preach Christ from less-than-the-best motives (Philippians 1:15). Yet he continued his ministry in Rome (1:13) and beyond through writing Ephesians, Philippians, Colossians, and Philemon during those months.

But having a great apostle imprisoned along with the uncertainty of how the matter would be resolved had a devastating effect on some of the believers. Undoubtedly many were praying for Paul during those months, especially for a quick and favorable resolution of his case. But God did not answer their prayers the way they wanted them answered. In effect, God said, "Not now." So Paul urged them not to lose heart because of his trouble. Even this delay was for their glory, for it would help them experience the super-superabundant power of God to sustain them when prayer was not answered at the time or in the way they wished. Paul also was indirectly reminding the Gentile readers of Ephesians that he was in confinement because he had proclaimed that God was bringing Gentiles into a relationship of equality with Jews in the body of Christ. This certainly was for their glory too.

To sum up: We glorify God in the church when we do not lose heart when our prayers are not answered as quickly as we would like; but instead we continue to persist in prayer.

(2) *Making Christ feel at home in our lives.* Paul next prays that believers might have the ability to be strengthened so that Christ might dwell in their hearts (Ephesians 3:16-17). Of course, the Lord lives within every believer (1 Corinthians 6:19-20), but the idea here is that He might dwell in a settled way in our lives—that He might feel "at home" in us. For one to feel at home in someone's house requires that he or she feels comfortable with the activities and lifestyle he finds in that household. For our Lord to feel at home in our lives He must feel comfortable with our attitudes and ambitions and actions and lifestyle. He cannot compromise Himself by changing His stan-

dards to conform to ours. Rather, we must change whatever is necessary to conform to what pleases Him so that He will feel comfortable with us. And that takes super-superabundant power to accomplish, for our hearts are rebellious, our wills stubborn, and our perspective too often earthly. We must be transformed to conform to His standards.

(3) *Comprehending the love of Christ.* Paul then prays that the believers may be able to comprehend the breadth and length and depth and height of the love of Christ. The breadth of God's love relates to His including Gentiles and Jews together in the one new man (Ephesians 2:15). There is no one who belongs to any race who cannot know the love of God. The length of His love extends from eternity past throughout all eternity future (1:4; 3:21). There never was, is, or will be a time when we cannot know the love of God. The height of God's love extends to the sphere of the heavenlies (1:3). This refers to the realm of heavenly possessions and experience into which the Christian has been brought because of his association with the risen Christ. The depth of God's love was great enough to be able to reach to us in our sinful, fallen condition (2:1, 12).

To comprehend all this takes the super-superabundant power of God.

(4) *Becoming mature.* Paul's fourth concern results from knowing the love of Christ. We are "to be filled up to the fullness of God" (verse 19, not "with," as some translations have, but "to"). What does this phrase mean? It refers to the maturing of the believer. The fullness of God is our standard (4:13), and continual growth and maturity is the way of progressing toward that standard. This too necessitates the super-superabundant power of God.

Now these four requests—not to be discouraged when we pray, to let Christ feel at home in our lives, to be able to comprehend the love of Christ, and to mature to the fullness of God—precede the great doxology in verses 20-21. So when we do these things through the super-superabundant power of God, then there is glory in the church and in Christ Jesus.

Notice that Paul does not say that the superability of God produces great success or usefulness because of what we *accomplish*, but rather it produces great maturity by changing and developing our *character*. Obviously if Christ feels at home in my life and the fullness of Christ is my goal in life, then my life will be transformed toward Christlikeness. I can then show to the world and the church the glory of God and His abundant ability to develop these traits in my life as I am transformed by these great truths. I will show glory to Him because He is able to do these things in my life, and my transformed and changing life proves it.

We must not fail to notice that there exists a corporate aspect to glorifying God in these ways. This glorifying is "in the church." But, of course, the church consists of individuals, so it must first be seen in individual lives; then the corporate aspect will be seen as well. This is biblical and basic "church growth"—a concept seldom, if ever, heard in church-growth seminars. But we know that patience and persistence in prayer, the rule of Christ in our hearts, the understanding of His love, and our spiritual maturity pleases and glorifies Him who is able by His super-superabundant power to develop these traits in our lives and thus in the church.

Now unto Him who is able to do exceedingly abundantly above all that we ask or think, according to the power that works in us, unto Him be glory in the church by Christ Jesus throughout all ages, world without end. Amen.

Ephesians 3:20-21

93

Chapter Nine

TO THE PRAISE OF HIS GLORY

That He might make known
the riches of His glory
on vessels of mercy
which He had previously prepared
for glory.

Wherefore receive one another,
as Christ also received us
to the glory of God.

Romans 9:23; 15:7

THE GLORY OF GOD, AS WE HAVE SEEN THROUGHOUT this book, means God displayed or revealed in any or all of His characteristics. To praise means to approve, to esteem, or to agree. In Ephesians 1:12 Paul wrote that we believers "should be to the praise of His glory." In other words we should exhibit high esteem for God's character.

But how can we be "to the praise of His glory"? Other Scriptures, like 1 Corinthians 10:31-32, indicate that we do this by the conduct of our lives, by *what we do for Him.* However, in Ephesians 1 we show esteem for who God is because of *what He has done for us.* In other words, He does some stupendous things for us which in turn make us praise or show high estimation for His person. Also in Ephesians 1 there are practical ramifications of these things which should transform our lives so that they will bring praise to His glory.

We Praise His Glory Because of What the Father Has Done for Us

According to Ephesians 1:4-6 He has done three great things for us.

(1) *He has chosen us* (verse 4). On what basis did He choose us? Certainly not because we were worthy of being chosen or because God could find something in us that would move Him to choose us. He chose us just because He wanted to. The voice of the verb indicates that God's choice was not forced by any consideration except His own desire to do it.

When did He choose us? Before the foundation of the world. Obviously that means also before we were born, before we

97

could exhibit any traits that would either commend us to God or
not. "So then, it is not of him who wills, nor of him that runs,
but of God that shows mercy" (Romans 9:16).

Why did He choose us? In order that we should be holy and
blameless before Him. Peter uses both these words in 1 Peter
1:16, 19. Our holiness is measured against the standard of God's
holiness. Our blamelessness is also measured against the
blamelessness of Christ, the Lamb of God. He chose us so that
our transformed lives can display holiness and blamelessness.
To be holy and blameless is to be like God and like Christ.
Because He wants us to be like Himself, He chose us to be in
His family.

God's pretemporal choice of His people is not something to
fear but something to demonstrate in holy and blameless lives,
lives that are like Christ's. In this way we show how much we
esteem His character because we want our character to conform
as much as possible to His. We should bear the likeness of the
family into which we have come. Whatever characteristics our
Heavenly Father has, we should also show.

(2) *He has adopted us as sons* (verse 5). Adoption places the
believer in the Father's family as a member with full adult
privileges belonging to that position. At the same time, when
one is adopted, all previous relationships and responsibilities
related to any former family end.

Adoption was a very common aspect of Greek and Roman life
though it was not incorporated as a part of Jewish law. This was
probably due to the fact that the Old Testament law provided a
way for a family to have heirs to inherit the family property.
That provision was levirate marriage, in which a childless widow
wed her brother-in-law if he was available (Deuteronomy 25:5-
6). But in Greek and Roman culture childless couples would
often adopt a son who then became their heir. Even if the
adopted son had living biological parents, they had no more
claim over him once the adoption had taken place.

In this verse Paul says that God's predetermined plan included our destiny as adopted sons. Like choosing us, adopting us is also a voluntary act on the part of the Father. And, too, like being chosen to be holy and blameless, people who are adopted into God's family should behave like members of His family.

(3) *He has graced us with grace in Christ* (verse 6). "Favored" or "freely given" in this verse translates the verb "to grace." This verb is used in only one other place in the New Testament—Luke 1:28. There the Angel Gabriel greeted Mary and said that she was "highly favored," or literally, "graced." Every believer has been graced or accepted in Christ, something no one could do on his or her own.

These blessings which the Father has given us show how highly esteemed the display of His grace is, and in turn how highly we should esteem Him for doing these miraculous things.

We Praise His Glory Because of What the Son Has Done for Us

According to Ephesians 1:7-12, Jesus Christ has also accomplished great things for us.

(1) *He has provided redemption for us* (verse 7). The New Testament writers use three principal words to describe our redemption. The basic word *agorazo* ("to purchase") includes three ideas: Christ paid the price of our redemption (2 Peter 2:1); that price was His own blood (Revelation 5:9-10); and because we have been bought with that price, we are to serve Him (1 Corinthians 6:19-20).

The second word for redemption, *exagorazo,* is a compound of the first and adds the idea of purchasing out of the market where goods were bought and sold (Galatians 3:13; 4:5).

The third word, *lutroo,* from the root "to loose," adds the idea of release of the purchased item or object. This is the word (in a compound form) used in Ephesians 1:7. Christ has redeemed us—

99

paid the price, removed us from the marketplace of sin, and released us to live for His glory.

(2) *He has provided forgiveness* (verse 7). Forgiveness means a releasing, a releasing from the condemnation of our sins. Forgiveness wipes the slate clean. Forgiveness lifts the burden that our sins lay upon us. And it is the One against whom we have sinned who Himself forgives us.

(3) *He gives us an understanding of His plan* (verses 8-12). This understanding involves knowing the mystery of His will and the inheritance we have in Christ. The mystery is the inclusion of Jews and Gentiles in the one new body of Christ (2:14-16). To a Gentile living in the time of our Lord that would have seemed an impossible accomplishment. A Gentile had no assurance of acceptance with God unless he became a proselyte to Judaism. That involved being circumcised, being baptized, and offering sacrifices. But now suddenly God opened a *new way* to Himself for both Jews and Gentiles and a *new membership*, not in Judaism, but in the body of Christ. It was not only a miracle that Gentiles could come to God but also that Jewish people could come in this new way. The "we" in verse 11 likely refers to Jews; i.e., Jews have now obtained an inheritance in Christ. What an amazing tribute to the glory of God—and what a call to praise—that Jews and Gentiles can now be united in the body of Christ.

We Praise His Glory for What the Holy Spirit Has Done for Us

Back in verse 11 Paul links our receiving the inheritance with being predestined. But predestination does not of itself save. Faith does (verses 12-13). Even a predestined person has to believe in order to be saved.

Once we have believed, the Holy Spirit does two things for us. He seals us and He Himself becomes the pledge or earnest of the inheritance God has provided (verse 14).

The concept of being sealed includes several ideas. In this passage sealing primarily means security, and security until the day we arrive in heaven, the day of our full redemption (4:30). Security also seems to be the meaning in Matthew 27:66 which records the securing of our Lord's tomb after His death. This was probably done by attaching a cord to the stone and then connecting it to the tomb with wax or clay. Today when we seal an envelope we expect its contents to be secure. If we want more security then we register the letter or package at the post office where additional measures are taken to ensure its safe and secure arrival. Similarly, the presence of the Holy Spirit in our lives is God's seal which guarantees our safe arrival in heaven some day.

Sealing also involves the ideas of approval (John 6:27), authentication (John 3:33), and ownership (2 Corinthians 1:22; Revelation 7:2). To some extent each of these ideas may be seen in this Ephesians passage as well. A God who can seal frail, sinning, unreliable children, such as we all are, and guarantee our future in heaven is certainly One whose glory is to be esteemed highly. To be sure, we esteem Him for what He has done, but more than that we esteem Him for being the kind of God who can and wishes to do these things for us.

How does this act of sealing transform us? By constantly reminding us that we have a relationship with the Holy Spirit who is grieved when we sin. This should motivate us to purer lives, especially in the area of our speech (note that the verses immediately preceding and following Ephesians 4:30 highlight sins of the tongue).

The Holy Spirit serves also as the pledge or earnest of our inheritance. His presence in our lives guarantees that eventually the full inheritance will be ours. The Spirit in us becomes a foretaste of much more to come when we arrive in heaven in the presence of God.

Suppose I were to ask you if you would like to have my gold watch. I am not proposing to give it to you, but I will sell it to you if you will give me a fair price for it.

What would you offer me for it? (And you name an amount.)

Too little. If you will offer me a little more, I will sell it to you. (And you up the price.)

OK. We have a deal.

But you say that you do not have all the money just now and it will be a month or two before you do.

No problem. Just give me part of the money now as a pledge or earnest that when you get the full amount you will complete the transaction.

So, I take your pledge money, and by giving it to me you guarantee to give me the rest in a month or two. By receiving your money I guarantee to take care of the watch so that you can have it in good condition when you pay me the rest of the purchase price.

God's gift of the Holy Spirit to reside in our lives while we live here on earth guarantees that He will also give us the remainder of our inheritance. His presence is just a taste or sample of all that awaits us in heaven. The Spirit also is God's pledge that God will not back out of the transaction or default in any way on His promises.

Do you know what specific facet of God's character this reveals? Immutability, which means that God is unchangeable and unchanging (Malachi 3:6; James 1:17). And since He is, we can be certain that He will not default on any of the great works He has done for us.

 But my part of the pledge binds me to keep myself in good condition before God. Like the watch, I am going to try to keep myself in good order during all the days of my life until I arrive in heaven.

All of these blessings are to the praise of His glory. Again, we do not esteem God's character only because He does all of these awesome things for us, but because He is the God who can and wishes to do them. God's glory is certainly seen in His works, and we esteem Him for them. But behind the works must be a Being who can produce them. And our high esteem is ultimately for the Person and all the facets of His character.

Grace be with all those
who love our Lord Jesus Christ
in sincerity.

Ephesians 6:24

Chapter Ten

BEARING MUCH FRUIT TO THE GLORY OF GOD

—————

And this I pray,
that your love may abound yet
more and more in knowledge
and discernment;
that you may prove excellent things,
that you may be sincere and unoffending
in the day of Christ,
having been filled with the
fruit of righteousness
through Jesus Christ,
to the glory and praise of God.

Philippians 1:9-11

—————

OUR LORD SAID: "IF YOU ABIDE IN ME, AND MY WORDS abide in you, you shall ask what you wish, and it shall be done unto you. In this is My Father glorified, that you bear much fruit; so shall you prove to be My disciples" (John 15:7-8).

By a fruitful life, the Christian glorifies God.

[handwritten margin notes: I am responsibility for the depth (abiding ...) He will provide the breadth]

The Nature of Fruit

What is fruit? Or better phrased, what are fruits which the believer can produce?

More than once the question has been answered this way: Fruit is any work of the Holy Spirit in the life of the believer. Now, I think that is a true answer, but it is certainly not very specific and does not help me to know whether I am being fruitful or not. Actually the New Testament does give us particulars about fruit.

As we survey the passages which deal with fruit, we notice that they fall into two general categories: (1) Some passages link fruit with developing a Christian character. Notice especially Galatians 5:22-23 and 2 Peter 1:5-8. (2) Others concern good works which we do that produce fruit for God's glory. Paul prayed, as recorded in Colossians 1:10, that believers might be fruitful in every good work. Other passages which concern good works we will examine later.

Christian Character

First, a developing Christian character is fruit. Since the goal of our lives is Christlikeness, then every trait developed and seen in

107

us that reflects Christ's character must be fruit and the kind of fruit that pleases Him. Paul describes the fruit of the Spirit in nine terms in Galatians 5:22-23, and Peter urges the development of seven accompaniments to faith in order that we might be fruitful (2 Peter 1:5-8). Two of these traits are common to both lists: love (a self-sacrificing desire to seek what is good for the one loved) and self-control (of one's passions). The others are joy (a sense of well-being rooted in our relation with God), peace (tranquility), long-suffering (evenness under provocation), kindness (benevolent action), goodness (kind thoughts and actions), faithfulness (reliability), meekness (gentleness), virtue (moral excellence), knowledge (spiritual wisdom), endurance (staying-power under adversity), piety (reverence toward God), and brotherly love (caring for others). When we exhibit and develop these traits in our lives then we are bearing fruit. Primarily, these are character traits, not activities, although if the Christlike characteristics are present then they will surely affect and transform our actions.

Good Works

Second, a life of good works is a fruitful life (Colossians 1:10). What good works specifically?

(1) *Witnessing.* Leading people to salvation in Christ is fruit (Romans 1:13). Although the church at Rome was not one of those founded by Paul, he nevertheless wanted, more than once, to visit there "in order to have some fruit" among the people as he had among other Gentiles. A few years later Paul did get to Rome, and we know of at least one person, presumably among many others, whom he led to Christ—the slave Onesimus (Philemon 10).

In another place Paul calls the household of Stephanus the "firstfruits of Achaia" (1 Corinthians 16:15). This simply means that Stephanus' family members were among the first converts in the region of central and southern Greece. Furthermore, these new converts took upon themselves the work of ministering to others, and Paul encouraged the Corinthians to submit to them. Verse 17 indicates that Stephanus was apparently one of those who brought the report and questions from this church at Corinth to Paul, his response to which is contained elsewhere in 1 Corinthians (see 7:1).

(2) *Giving.* We bear fruit when we give money. Paul labeled the collection he was making for the poor believers in Jerusalem as fruit (Romans 15:28). In addition, when he thanked the Philippians for the gift of money they had sent to him for his ministry, he said that their act of giving brought fruit to their account (Philippians 4:17, kjv).

(3) *Praising.* We may also bear fruit with our lips by giving praise to God and thankfully confessing His name (Hebrews 13:15). The peace offering of the Old Testament stands in the background of this verse. One of the uses of this offering (of an unblemished male or female ox, lamb, or goat) was as a sacrifice of thanksgiving (Leviticus 7:12). In the New Testament economy our lips replace the sacrificial animal, and with them we offer our sacrifice of thanksgiving. When our lips are fruitful they will confess His name. That simply means that we acknowledge all that God is to us—all that His name stands for. Every believer can certainly bear this kind of fruit. Note that the writer says that we should praise always, not sporadically.

Increasing the Yield

In the principal passage on fruitbearing, John 15, our Lord told His disciples (Judas having previously left the group) that He had appointed them to go and bear lasting fruit (verse 16), and in the preceding verses He told them how.

(1) *By encouragement.* First, if we are fruitless we need to respond to the Vinedresser's encouragement (John 15:2). An

interpretive question exists concerning the meaning of the first part of verse 2. Who are the fruitless branches? Do they indicate professing believers or genuine believers? Some understand them to be professing believers who outwardly associate with the church but who have never personally received Christ as Savior. If one believes in eternal security then verse 6 would seem to support this interpretation. In other words, since true believers are eternally secure, then the branches that are taken away (verse 2) or are cast into the fire (verse 6) must be professing believers, since true believers cannot be taken away or cast into the fire. Of course, if one does not hold that believers are eternally secure, then both verses can refer to genuine believers who do lose their salvation.

But others (myself included) understand that the fruitless believers in verse 2 are genuine believers since they are said to be in Christ and also since the Lord was conversing only with the remaining eleven disciples. If this is the correct interpretation, then what does the Vinedresser do to fruitless believers?

In answering that question another interpretive question arises. The verb in the first part of verse 2 *(airo)* means both "to take away or remove" and "lift up." In John's Gospel the verb is translated both ways. In John 5:8 it is correctly translated "take up." Yet in John 1:29 it is also correctly translated "take away." If it means "take away" in John 15:2, and if the reference is to genuine believers, then the Lord is saying that God may remove fruitless believers from this earth through physical death. This makes it a similar warning to that in verse 6.

But if we understand the verb to mean that He lifts up fruitless believers, then the idea is that God encourages the fruitless believer to bear fruit by exposing him or her to God's goodness.

So, according to the interpretation that these are fruitless believers, the Gardener removes them in judgment or, more likely, in my opinion, He lifts them up in help and blessing, positioning them to bear fruit as they respond to His encouragement.

(2) *By pruning.* Second, the Father prunes those branches that are bearing fruit so that they may bear more fruit (verse 2). What does pruning mean? Simply that our wise and loving Heavenly Father removes all useless things that would sap the strength of the branch and keep it from bearing more fruit. Constant pruning is necessary if the fruit is to grow to full maturity. Similarly in our lives, our Father removes unhelpful things, useless things, and harmful things. Such could include disciplining us (Hebrews 12:6-11), bringing into our lives physical limitations (2 Corinthians 12:7-10), allowing material reverses and losses (Hebrews 10:34), permitting family losses (James 1:27), and exposing us to unjustified persecution (1 Peter 4:12-16). Whatever it may take, our Heavenly Father wisely does in order that we may bear more fruit.

The word that is translated "prune" in verse 2 *(kathairo)* is the same root word that is translated "clean" in verse 3. And these processes of pruning or cleansing come, according to verse 3, because of the Word of God. The teachings of our Lord had already cleansed the Eleven, and they would continue to cleanse all other believers also. The Word of God constitutes an inseparable instrument in pruning and cleansing.

(3) *By abiding.* Third, abiding in Christ is necessary in order that we might bear much fruit (verses 4-10). Not satisfied with branches that are bearing more fruit, the Gardener longs that they may bear much fruit. And the path to that goal is abiding or remaining in Christ.

What does it mean to abide in Christ? In simplest terms it means to keep His commandments. According to verse 10 the Lord said: "If you keep My commandments, you shall abide in My love." John reiterated the same definition in 1 John 3:24: "And he who keeps His commandments abides in Him, and He in him." Such a definition makes good sense, for the more we obey Him the more we remain in Him. When we disobey by failing to keep His commandments, then we move ourselves away from Him

111

rather than abiding in Him. The one who keeps God's commandments or Word will bear much fruit simply because he or she will be doing those things which please God.

Abiding also brings another important result: answered prayer (John 15:7). Besides being biblical, this idea is logical. The one who keeps God's commandments knows best what to pray for and will then pray in the will of God. And prayers in the will of God will be answered. If we abide in Him (keep His commandments), and His words abide in us (increasing knowledge of and obedience to the Word of God), we can ask what we wish (for we will want to ask what is His will), and He will answer. And answered prayers bring three results (verse 8): (1) the Father is glorified; (2) we bear much fruit; (3) we show or prove ourselves to be His disciples.

Let me illustrate this relationship between answered prayer and glorifying God by a personal experience.

Years ago when I traveled abroad to do graduate work, I discovered that one did not simply buy a plane ticket and go. Preparations had to be made before leaving the country—shots, passport, visa, some way to take care of personal affairs at the home base as well as to get money to live on while away. If a person owned property or had loans, then some arrangement had to be made to make the payments on those loans and to pay taxes and insurance on the property, collect the rent, and take care of things in general. All those matters you would normally take care of yourself have to be cared for by someone in your absence.

To accomplish all this I signed a document called a power of attorney. This authorized my attorney (in this case, my father) to do anything in my name and on my behalf. Sometimes a power of attorney can be given for one specific thing or for several, but in this case it was for everything. My attorney could borrow money in my name and, of course, I would have been liable for the debt. He could have sold any property I might have owned. He could have played the stock market.

112

He could have taken an expensive vacation for himself and signed my name to the checks to pay for it. He could have done anything.

But, although I gave my attorney blanket power, I never feared that I had also given him a blank check, for I knew that he would never do anything I would not approve of or stand behind. And when he did those things that had to be done, my reputation was kept intact, even enhanced. When my lenders saw payments coming in regularly from my attorney on my behalf, they were pleased, especially because they knew that even though I was out of the country, I had made the necessary arrangements to take care of those payments. My attorney did the job, but I was the one who received the thanks and the glory.

If we keep Christ's commandments and if His words abide in us, then we will pray only for those matters which are according to His will. And when our prayers are answered, it is not we who receive the glory—as if we brought those answers to pass—but our Heavenly Father. We are attorneys who do the job of praying according to His will and desires, and He is the One who arranges all the factors involved in the answers and who therefore receives the glory.

Progression marks this John 15 passage. Response to God's goodness can move us from fruitlessness to fruitfulness. Pruning, difficult as it may be, can move us from fruitfulness to more fruitfulness. Abiding, particularly as it relates to answered prayer, can produce much fruit in our lives.

But progression also has an opposite: retrogression. Just as believers can progress, they can also retrogress from any stage of fruitfulness. Very fruitful believers can retrogress to bearing less fruit and presumably can even slide back to a fruitless condition at least for some period of time. Disobedience to God's Word brings retreat in the spiritual life, just as obedience results in progress.

Verse 6 warns strongly against disobedience (that is, not abiding in Christ), and the barrenness which will result. Such believers will lose further opportunities to bear fruit. At what point in their pilgrimage this loss may occur cannot be predicted, but it can and does happen. If and when this happens, their branch (spiritual fruitfulness) withers. And if the barrenness continues unchecked, these believers will lose rewards at the Judgment Seat of Christ. Paul describes their works as wood, hay, and straw, for which there will be no reward. And yet they will be saved (1 Corinthians 3:15). John also wrote of the real possibility of losing one's full reward (2 John 8).

How important it is for God's glory that we bear much fruit. And bearing much fruit is largely a private matter. Certainly Christlike character is developed individually and privately. Witnessing can be done in many ways, both publicly and privately. Praising God can be done in private and in public. When we give, the Lord told us not to let our left hand know what our right hand is doing. Studying the Bible so that we know how to abide in Christ is largely a private discipline, though it may be aided by public ministry. And certainly prayer should be more private than public.

What a goal—to be fruitful to the praise of His glory!

Now the God of all grace, who has called us to His eternal glory in Christ, after you have suffered a while, will perfect, confirm, strengthen, and establish you. To Him be glory and dominion forever and ever. Amen.

1 Peter 5:10-12

Chapter Eleven

PREVIEWS OF COMING GLORY

———————————

We rejoice in the hope of the glory of God.

For I consider that the sufferings
of this present time
are not worth comparing with the glory
that will be revealed to us.

Romans 5:2; 8:18

———————————

YOU KNOW HOW HOLLYWOOD DOES IT. PREVIEWS OF the networks' new shows for the coming season. And what do they show on these previews? Just the most exciting or intriguing glimpses so that you will hopefully be enticed to tune in when they are aired.

Christ's Transfiguration—A Preview of Things To Come

Our Lord did this sort of thing, only about something far more significant than a new television program. He had told His disciples about His approaching death—that it would involve suffering, that it would be at the hands of the leaders of the nation (the elders, chief priests, and scribes), that it would be in Jerusalem, and that He would rise from the dead on the third day (Luke 9:22). He also predicted that some of the disciples would not die before seeing the kingdom of God. And this prophecy was fulfilled to Peter, James, and John when, just a week later, the Lord was transfigured before their very eyes on a mountain as He prayed.

The Place of the Transfiguration

The mountain on which this momentous event occurred was likely Mount Hermon in the north of Palestine. It stood near Caesarea Philippi, the area in which Peter had just made his great confession of Christ as the Son of the Living God. The mountain's great height (9,232 feet above sea level) and privacy make it the best candidate (others being Mount Tabor, the Mount of Olives, and Jebel Jarmuk in Upper Galilee).

117

The Concept of "Transfiguration"

Having gone to the mountain our Lord began to pray, and while He was praying He was transformed. Matthew (17:2) and Mark (9:2) both record that He was transfigured, while Luke says that His face was different (9:29). The New Testament uses the word *transfigured* (similar to our English word *metamorphosis)* in three connections. Here it refers to the change that came over Christ's appearance on the mountain. It also describes what ought to be the believer's experience in progressive sanctification as he or she is changed into the likeness of Christ by the Holy Spirit (2 Corinthians 3:18). This is also the same transformation which we should experience as we reject conformity to this world and renew our minds so as to know and do the will of God (Romans 12:2).

The Lessons Learned from the Appearance of
Moses and Elijah

Only Luke adds a detail about the appearance of Moses and Elijah which teaches us something concerning existence after death. Luke says that Moses and Elijah appeared "in glory" (Luke 9:31). This seems not to be a reference to our Lord's glory but to some glory they themselves had. Peter, James, and John saw Moses and Elijah in a splendorous glory.

"Appearing in glory" suggests an intriguing question about the body a believer has between death and resurrection. When a believer dies his spirit goes immediately to be with the Lord (2 Corinthians 5:8). His body is disposed of in some manner here on earth. Apparently no believer will receive a resurrection body until the Lord comes. So both at the rapture of the church and at the second coming of Christ those who have died previous to these events will be raised, changed, and will receive their eternal bodies of glory. At that time believers will receive bodies that will be conformed (same root word as is in *transfigure)* to His body (Philippians 3:21).

But in the meantime (between death and resurrection) with what sort of body is the spirit clothed in heaven?

Moses and Elijah would not have had their final glorified bodies at the time of the Transfiguration. But they were in heaven and their appearance was glorious. This tells us two things. First, Moses was not waiting in some "saved compartment" of sheol or hades until after Christ died so that He might take all those Old Testament believers in that "compartment" to heaven during the three days between His death and resurrection. This so-called two-compartment theory developed during the period between the Old and New Testaments (though reinforced, some say, by the account of the rich man and Lazarus in Luke 16:19-31, especially verse 23).

Second, we learn that even in heaven, between death and resurrection, those in heaven appear "in glory." Is this a hint about the nature of what is often called "the intermediate body"? Some think Paul refers to that intermediate body in 2 Corinthians 5:1-4, while others feel he is speaking of the final resurrection body of believers. In any case, we know that Moses, who died and whose body was buried (Deuteronomy 34:5-6), but whose spirit went to heaven, and Elijah, who did not die but who was taken directly to heaven (2 Kings 2:11-18), both appeared in that intermediate time in splendorous glory. And so shall we, while we wait in His presence between death and resurrection. What a preview! What an assurance!

But whatever we may or may not know about the intermediate body, we do know that when Christ is revealed then we also will be revealed with Him in glory (Colossians 3:4). Glory will then be ours, specifically, among other things, with a body conformed to the body of His glory (Philippians 3:21). But also we shall be "like Him" (1 John 3:2). What does it mean to be like Him? Certainly not carbon copies, for He is the great God and

119

Creator, and we are creatures forever. But John, I believe, explains what to be "like Him" means in the context of 1 John 3:2. Being "like Him" includes our being pure, for He is pure (verse 3). It means being without sin, for in Him is no sin (verse 5). And it assures our being righteous, for He is righteous (verse 7). What a future lies ahead for all believers—guaranteed by His Word!

The Lessons about the Future

(1) *The centrality of Christ's death.* The disciples accompanying Jesus at the Transfiguration learned about the necessity and centrality of our Lord's death. Earlier the Lord had predicted His approaching death (Luke 9:22), and Matthew records how Peter responded with total disbelief (Matthew 16:22). Death won't happen to you, Peter insisted. The Lord's response was even stronger, for He addressed Peter as Satan. Why? Simply because Peter had sided with Satan's plan to keep Christ from going to the cross to die for the sins of the world. Our Lord's death on the cross was central and absolutely necessary to atone for sin.

Moses and Elijah were talking about the Lord's death (Luke 9:30-31). Luke uses the word *exodus* to describe Christ's approaching death in Jerusalem. Our Lord's exodus, that is, His death, would be that which would bring salvation to this world, just as Israel's exodus from Egypt brought freedom from bondage in Egypt. Israel's freedom was temporary and bound to the earthly land of Canaan. The believer's exodus is eternal and to an inheritance in heaven.

When Peter overheard Moses and Elijah speaking of Christ's "exodus" he apparently still did not understand that it was of Christ's death that they spoke. Hearing the word *exodus* caused him to think of the exodus of Israel from Egypt which was commemorated in the annual Feast of Booths (Leviticus 23:33-44). Remembering the significance of that event caused Peter to blurt out his idea to build three booths right then and there.

(2) *Suffering must precede death.* The disciples also learned that day about the sequence of suffering before glory. They already were assured that Christ would reign in glory in the future, and they glimpsed that glory on the Mount of Transfiguration. But His suffering and death had to come first. Nevertheless, their experience on this occasion made them more sure of the glory that would eventually be our Lord's. A generation later Peter wrote that the experience on the Mount of Transfiguration made the prophetic word more sure (2 Peter 1:16-19). And for us too the record of the Transfiguration confirms the truth of prophecies concerning the future and makes them even more sure from a human point of view. The future reign of our Lord in glory is guaranteed by the preview the disciples saw.

A Prayer Finally Answered

Do you remember Moses' prayer hundreds of years before this time that he might see God's glory? (Exodus 33:18) On that occasion, while Moses was still here on earth, God only showed Moses His back but not His face. Now on the Mount of Transfiguration after Moses had been in heaven for hundreds of years, he at last saw God's glory face-to-face, for all present that day saw the transfigured Christ's glory (Luke 9:32). And since He is God, they saw God's glory.

This incident reminds all of us that some requests that we make to God in prayer may not be granted in our lifetime. Sometimes we could not handle the answers even if they were to come within our lifetime. Even in eternity our questions as to why some of the things we requested were not granted may not be cleared up. Indeed, our understanding may take many ages of spiritual maturing to comprehend. In the meantime we trust the God who can be trusted fully. Even though we may not receive answers every time we ask the question, "Why?" we *can* ask,

"What shall we do in the problem or difficulty?" and our Father will likely tell us. Then we must obediently do whatever He says and trust Him even though we do not understand why something has happened.

We Learn about Heaven and the New Jerusalem

On the Mount of Transfiguration the disciples saw the glory of Christ (Luke 9:32), a preview of His and God's glory which will be exhibited in heaven forever.

Revelation 21–22 describes the New Jerusalem. Twice in that description John says that it has the glory of God (21:11, 23). What is this New Jerusalem? Almost all understand it to describe the characteristics of eternity. Some feel that Revelation 21:9-21 describes the New Jerusalem in relation to the Millennium. This would be no contradiction, for the New Jerusalem will be the home of the redeemed both in the Millennium and throughout eternity, and within the city eternal conditions will exist even though outside its wall temporal conditions will prevail during the Millennium.

What the New Jerusalem Is Like

The Lord promised that when He left this earth He was going to prepare a place for His people (John 14:3). The New Jerusalem seems to be a description of that place which will be our home forever. The writer to the Hebrews speaks of this heavenly Jerusalem as the abode of the saints (Hebrews 12:22-24).

What are some of the characteristics of the New Jerusalem?

(1) In it God will dwell with His people throughout eternity (Revelation 21:3).

(2) The sorrowful experiences of this present life will be eliminated (verses 4-5). No more tears, no more death, no more sorrow or pain.

(3) New experiences will replace the old ones (verses 6-7): full satisfaction ("the fountain of the water of life"), full inheritance, and full fellowship.

(4) Not everyone will be included in that place (verse 8). Those whose lifestyles have proved their hearts were never regenerated will be cast into the lake of fire forever.

How is the New Jerusalem described?

(1) It is a place where the glory of God shines like the brilliance of a very costly, crystal-clear precious stone (verse 11). This brilliance is the radiance of God's complete character, His glory, which will illumine the place.

(2) It also is a place of total security, for its high wall and angel-guards at its twelve gates will protect its inhabitants (verse 12).

(3) "Will it be large enough?" you might ask. A 1,380-mile cube, the New Jerusalem will cover an area equivalent to the size of the United States from Canada to the Gulf of Mexico and from Colorado to the Atlantic, allowing more than ample space to all its inhabitants. Dr. Henry Morris in *The Revelation Record* (Wheaton, Illinois: Tyndale House, 1983, p. 451) has made the following calculations: He figures that the total number of people since the time of Adam to the present is about 40 billion. To this figure he adds 20 billion for those who died before or soon after birth, and 40 billion more for the population of the Millennium, for a total of 100 billion people, past, present, and future. Assuming that 20 percent of this number are redeemed and therefore inhabitants of the New Jerusalem, and assuming that only 25 percent of the city will be used for dwellings, then each resident would have a cubical block of about 75 acres or one third of a mile on each side. Obviously there would still be plenty of room for many more believers. Places for another 20 billion would take up only another 25 percent of the space.

(4) The description in Revelation 21:18-21 exudes beauty as a characteristic of the New Jerusalem. Imagine the glory of God reflected by crystal-clear jasper and pure gold and the multi-

colored stones in the foundation and the pearls in the gates. The colors of the stones mentioned include blue, green, brown, red, yellow, and purple.

(5) The city does not require a temple or place of worship to provide access to God because God and the Lamb will be present and together they constitute the temple (verses 22-23).

(6) Life in heaven will be life at its very best, where we will enjoy the water of life and the tree of life forever (22:1-2).

(7) No curse and no evil will be present (verse 3); yet eternal life is no idle life merely to be lived free from the curse and presence of sin. It is a life of service for God throughout all eternity.

No wonder Paul wrote that the sufferings of the present time are not worthy to be compared with the glory that will be revealed in and to us (Romans 8:18). It will be revealed in us by all the changes that we will experience—including the wonderful truth that we will be like Him with bodies of glory. It will be revealed to us in the beauty of the surroundings of the New Jerusalem which is the glory of God, and in which glory we shall live forever and ever.

At home in the New Jerusalem which displays the effulgence and brilliance of the glory of God. At work in the service of the God of all glory forever and ever. This is our future by His grace.

We, according to His promise,
look for new heavens and a new earth,
in which dwells righteousness.
Wherefore, beloved,
seeing that you await such things,
be diligent that you may be found
by Him in peace, without spot,
and blameless.

2 Peter 3:13-14

The One who testifies
to these things says
"Yes, I am coming soon."
Amen!
Come, Lord Jesus.

Revelation 22:20

Chapter Twelve

TRANSFORMED
BY HIS GLORY

Ascribe to the Lord
O mighty ones,
ascribe to the Lord
glory and strength.
Give to the Lord
the glory due to His name;
Worship the Lord
for the splendor
of His holiness.

Psalm 29:1-2

WATCHING KIDS GROW UP PROVIDES AN EDUCATION
that cannot be gained in any other way.

Can you remember the time your children first became aware
of the significance of money, or have you observed this phenom-
enon in the children of others? In their earliest years money
means nothing to youngsters. They would play with it if you
would let them, but a $100 bill would be no more fun than a $1
bill. They have no sense of its value or use at that point in life.

But the day comes when children begin to realize that money
is not a plaything. Money buys things—things which they enjoy.
They also learn that there never seems to be enough to satisfy
their wants. Money begins to take on a value that they knew
nothing of earlier. As this stage of growth arrives, good parents
try to instill something of the worth of money, not only to buy
things that the family must have, but also to give to others who
do not have as much. We try to teach children not only that
money has intrinsic worth but that it can be squandered, saved,
used selfishly, or used wisely.

Children likely first learn the value of money by seeing what
it can do. What money their father and/or mother earns buys
the food on the table. It buys toys. It supports the church. It
furnishes toys and food to needy people at Christmas or times
of need.

Soon children want an allowance or chores for which they will
be paid—or both! They want to use money themselves, not just
watch how their parents use it. So we try to teach them how to
use money properly. Hopefully they will give some, save some,
and not spend it all on themselves. And when they are grown, we
hope they will have developed habits of thrift, generosity, and

selflessness in their use of whatever money God gives them.

How they use money will clearly show how they esteem it. Is it something to be used selfishly? Then they show that they esteem it only as a means of getting what they want. Do they use it wisely? Then they show that they esteem it for the true worth it has. That, in the finest sense, is being transformed by understanding the true worth of money.

The Greatness of God's Glory

The glory of God—God displayed—is a great gift to mankind in general and a munificent one to believers. It has intrinsic value, the worth of the person of our God Himself. We learn what the greatness of His glory is by coming to understand some of the stupendous things God has done in the world and for believers. Let me remind you of the things which we have seen in the previous chapters of this book.

Some Specifics for the World

(1) He created this universe to show His power, wisdom, and glory (Psalm 19:1-6; Romans 1:18-20).

(2) He holds the universe together so that it functions in an orderly and dependable way (Colossians 1:16-17).

(3) He governs the universe so as to bring everything to its God-ordained conclusion in spite of the opposition of Satan and rebellious human beings (Hebrews 1:2-3).

Man's response to this revelation of God's glory does not relate so much to the way he takes care of the world as it does to whether or not he allows the world to point him to the Creator. What he sees around him, in spite of the disruptions that occur, should make him consider that it could not have happened by chance, but only through the operation of a Being with great intelligence and power. This should lead him to weigh the strong possibility that there was a Creator who did it all. If he acknowledges that, possibly then he would also logically ask who this Creator is, and come to know the glory of God in Jesus Christ.

The glory of God displayed in the world should transform people from seeing themselves as "captains of their own fate" into penitent creatures who seek mercy from their Creator.

Some Specifics in the Old Testament

Moses saw the glory of God revealing His self-existence (in His name Yahweh), His presence (as Yahweh), His protection (the meaning of one of the words for grace), His strength (in His name El), His loyal love (the meaning of the other word for grace), and in His compassion, long-suffering, truthfulness, and forgiveness.

As a result, Moses bowed in worship, praising His glory. He had received a lavish revelation of God, and he responded properly.

We too, when we see the various facets of God's character, and especially His grace, can be transformed into those who acknowledge His worth in every aspect of our lives. We should be worshiping people in whatever we do.

The glory of God led the people of Israel as they moved through the wilderness. The presence of the cloud and fire above the tabernacle gave evidence of His presence under all circumstances, whether it was stationary or moving.

Ezekiel had a vision of God on His throne. He too fell on his face and worshiped, transformed by what He had seen. Later he again saw the glory of God, this time judging Israel for its sin by its removal from the temple and the city of Jerusalem. But once more he had a vision of the glory of God returning to the city and to the temple in blessing, something that is yet to occur during the millennial reign of Christ. Ezekiel learned that the glory or revelation of God can judge and bless. He and we praise and esteem both aspects of God's character.

Some Specifics in the Life of Christ

When His contemporaries saw the Lord Jesus, they saw the glory of God, even though it was heavily veiled. When we see Him in the Word what do we see? A Person who knew and trusted the Scriptures. A Person who prayed. A Person who always did the will of God. A Person who served others. A Person who loved sinners. If we truly recognize and esteem Him, then we will attempt to have our lives transformed so as to follow in His steps.

Some Specifics for the Believer

(1) Our position under the New Covenant brings us a far greater revelation of God's glory than was ever revealed under the Old Covenant, that is, the Mosaic Law. Our new relationship includes being liberated from the bondage of the old life and ways. It means we can be transformed stage by stage to reflect the glory of Christ in our lives.

(2) The New Covenant gives us a message of good news to proclaim to this world, and a perspective on this life to see it in comparison to the eternal weight of glory which we shall experience in the future. If we truly praise the glory which the New Covenant reveals to us, then we will pursue Christian growth and witness.

(3) God's plan of bringing us all together in the body of Christ praises His glory for only God could perform such a mighty miracle. If we esteem our position in the body of Christ, then we will praise the One who accomplished it — by not being discouraged when prayer seems not to be answered, by letting Christ feel at home in our lives, by trying to comprehend the love of Christ, and by maturing in our faith.

(4) For the believer God has done stupendous things. He chose us before the foundation of the world. He adopted us into

His family with full privileges. He begraced us in Christ, giving us the Holy Spirit as a pledge of our inheritance. Behind these tremendous accomplishments stands the God who can and wanted to do them. If we praise His glory we will endeavor to live as chosen, adopted, begraced members of His family.

(5) We glorify the Father when we bear much fruit. To do this involves being cleansed, abiding, and having prayers answered. In these ways we praise His glory and demonstrate it in spiritually productive lives.

Praising His glory means esteeming, approving, and giving recognition to Him, and this results in transformed lives.

Glorifying God in the Ordinary

When we think of Moses' or Ezekiel's experiences, or when we contemplate the great things God has done for believers in choosing, adopting, and placing us in the body of Christ, or when we think about the relationship of answered prayer to fruitfulness, our focus is on extraordinary things. But God particularly wants us to glorify Him in the ordinary affairs of life. No verse states that so well as 1 Corinthians 10:31: "Whether, therefore, you eat or drink; or whatever you do, do all to the glory of God."

First Corinthians 10:31 does not say, whether you try to avoid schisms (1:10), or whether you exercise church discipline (5:13b), or whether you have the right attitude toward marriage and the family (7:1-40), or whether you take the Lord's Supper in the right way (11:17-34), or whether you handle spiritual gifts properly (12:1–14:40), or whether you are orthodox about the resurrection (15:1-58), do all *these* things to the glory of God. We should, of course, glorify Him in everything, including these matters which Paul discusses in 1 Corinthians. But the focus of 10:31 is on glorifying Him in the ordinary matters of life, eating and drinking. We are all continually affected by the ordinary, and we are all responsible and accountable for how we handle the ordinary.

During my lifetime I have spoken at a number of dedications. Many involved the dedication of church buildings. It is not difficult to find appropriate texts for those dedicatory messages. Others involved missionaries about to embark on their careers. Again it is relatively easy to find the right texts for such occasions. Sometimes individuals wanted to affirm publicly their personal dedication. Again no problem with a suitable text. Once I spoke at the dedication of a library. I did not have to search too long for an appropriate passage to use (2 Timothy 4:13).

One time I was asked to speak at the dedication of a dining room at a summer camp. This was a difficult assignment for which to find an appropriate message text. What text did I use? First Corinthians 10:31. I pointed out how we Christians think of the glory of God much more easily when we go to church, or to the meetings at a Bible camp or conference, but glorifying God in a noisy dining room is another story.

Paul devotes three chapters in 1 Corinthians to discussing the spiritual ramifications of glorifying God in eating. Ordinary eating had become a spiritual problem.

Normally the Greeks and Romans offered the less desirable parts of an animal as sacrifices to their gods. They reserved the choicer cuts for themselves, eating them either at public banquets or at private dinners to which friends were invited.

What should a Christian do about such banquets? Could he go to the home of a friend and eat meat that had been offered to idols? Could he go to a heathen feast and eat meat that had been offered to idols? Could he buy meat at the market and eat it, knowing that the meat had been offered to idols? These were important questions that affected the ordinary life of believers at Corinth.

What were Paul's answers? You can buy meat that has been offered to idols and eat it simply because an idol is nothing, and if you offer something to nothing you have not affected the offering (8:1-8). But do not eat at heathen religious festivals because the meat would have been offered to demons, and you

134

must not share in anything like that (10:14-22). However, you may eat at home (10:23-26), as well as at the home of an unbeliever, unless a weaker brother is present and questions your doing so (10:27-30).

A weaker brother is not someone who carps at the person who exercises his liberty, but he is one who is genuinely trying to advance in the Christian life but who does not yet feel he has liberty in certain areas. To stumble or trip up such a weaker brother requires that the weaker brother be moving. You cannot trip anyone who is sitting on the sidelines of the race hurling accusations at the runners. Yet Paul says that he would curb his own liberty to eat meat offered to idols for the sake of weaker brothers who might be hindered in their Christian walk if he did so (8:13).

In concluding his long discussion of this problem that affected the ordinary, Paul summarized by commanding (the verb *do* in 10:31 is an imperative) that we continually do (*it* is a present imperative) all (especially the ordinary) to the glory of God.

This general principle is particularized in three ways in the three verses that follow. (1) We glorify God when we do not give anyone cause to trip up in his Christian life (10:32). (2) We glorify God when we seek the good of others, which is above all that they be saved (10:33). (3) We glorify God when we imitate Christ (11:1).

What could be clearer? Of course we glorify God when we imitate our Lord, for He is God and the outflooding of God's glory (Hebrews 1:3).

So let's do it with lives that have been transformed by His glory.

Worthy is the Lamb that was slain to receive power and riches and wisdom and might and honor and glory and blessing.

To Him who sits on the throne, and to the Lamb, be blessing and honor and glory and dominion forever and ever.

Revelation 5:12, 13b

SCRIPTURE INDEX

138

SUBJECT INDEX